this book belongs to

. . . .

COLOR TEST PAGE

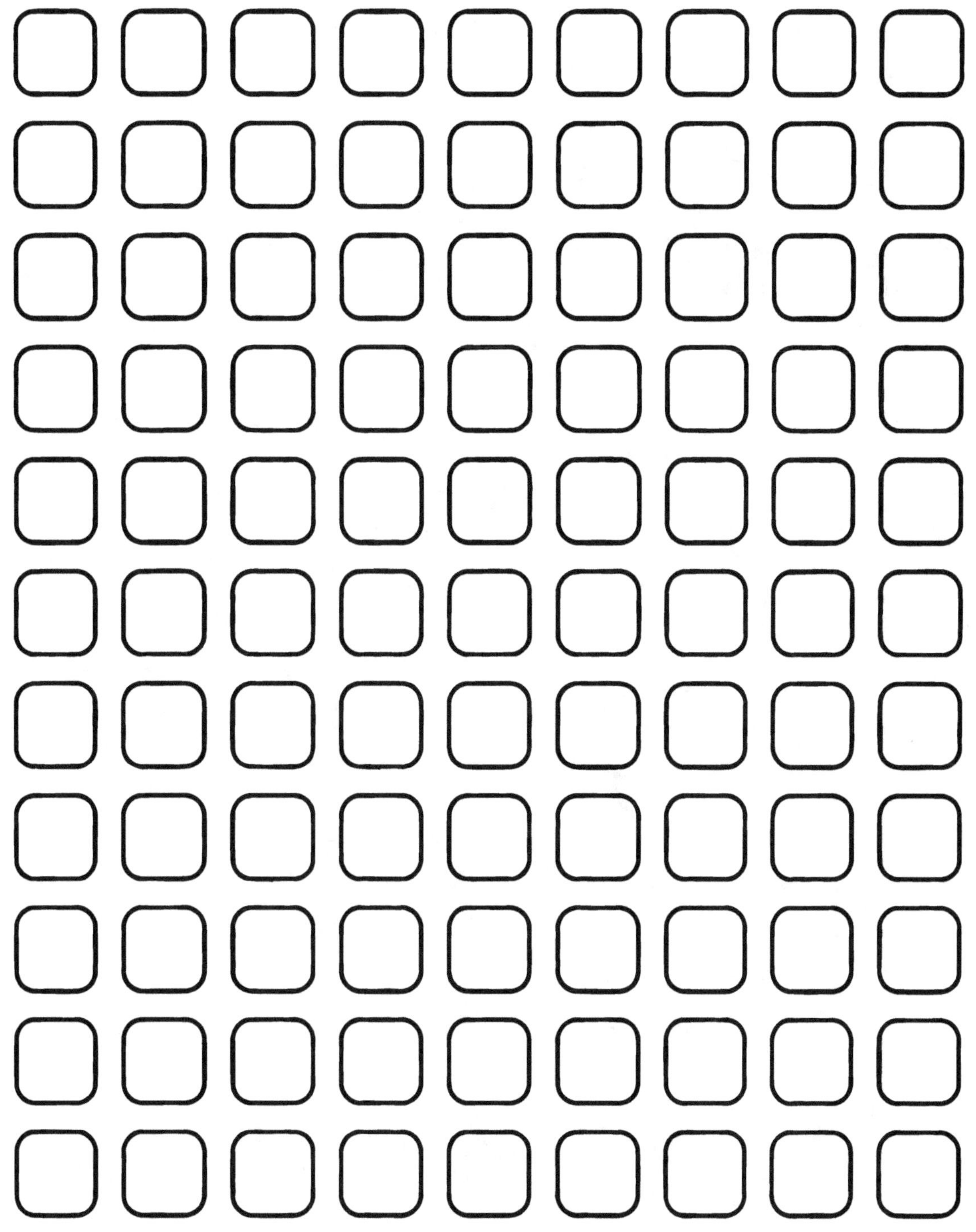

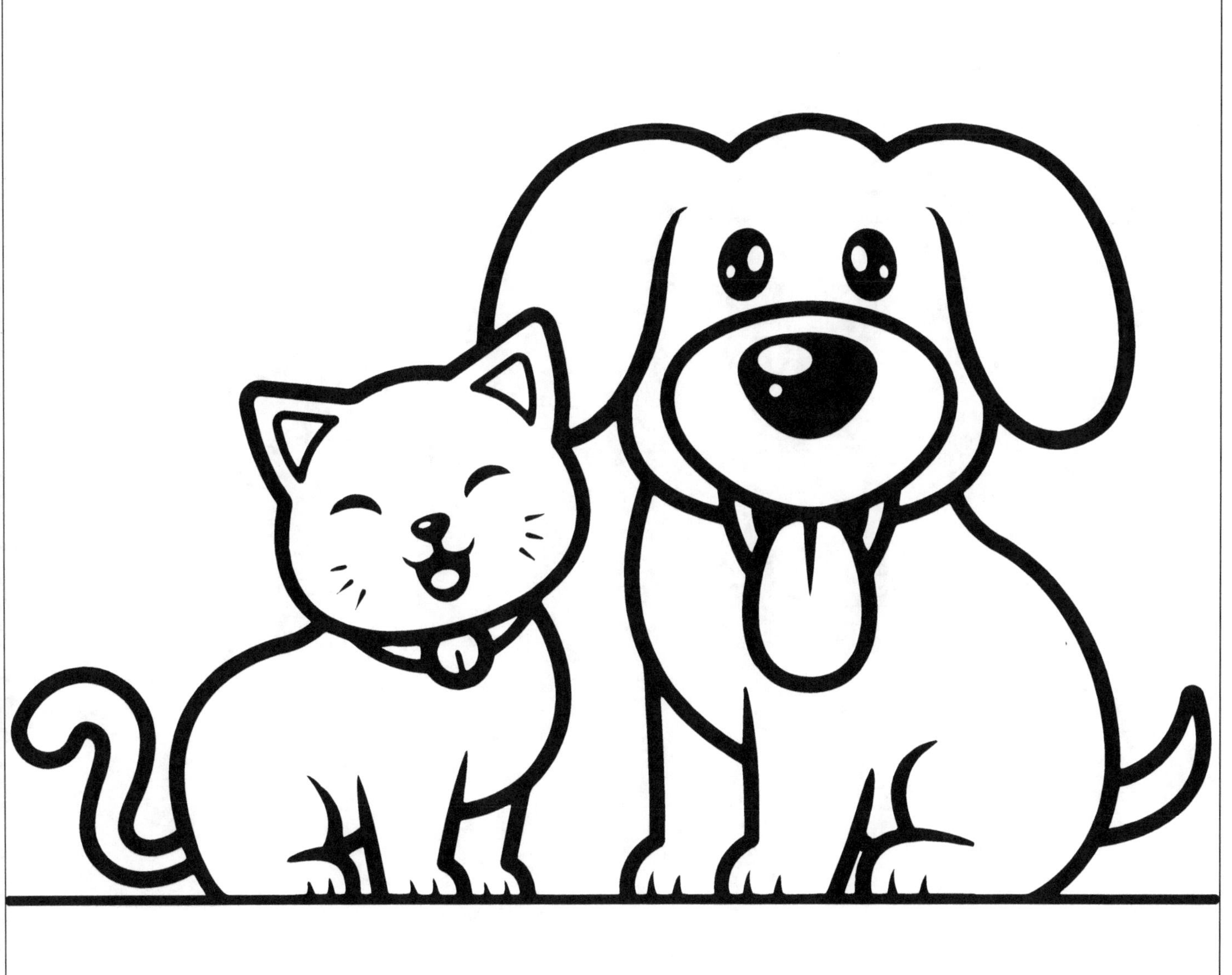

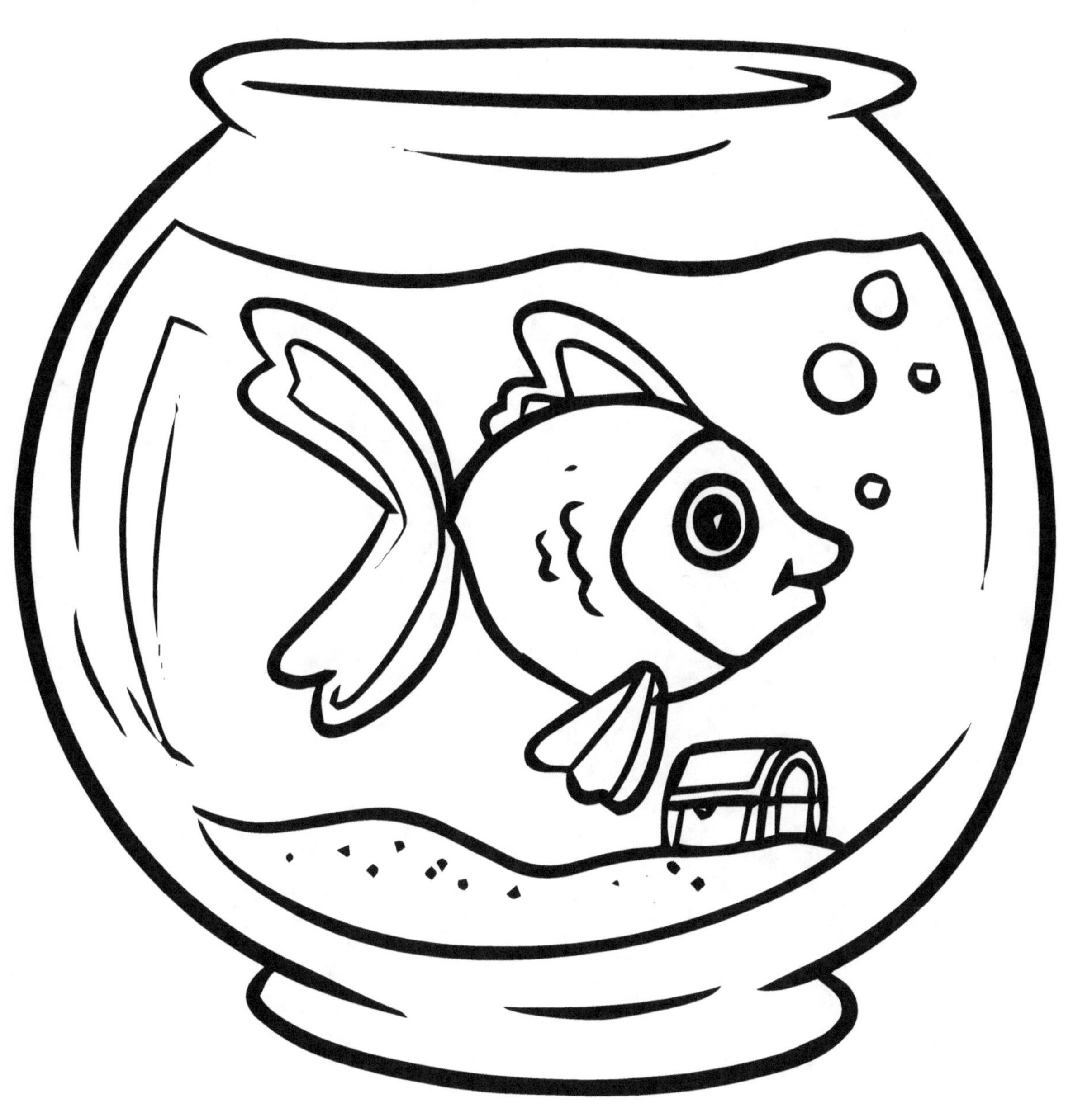

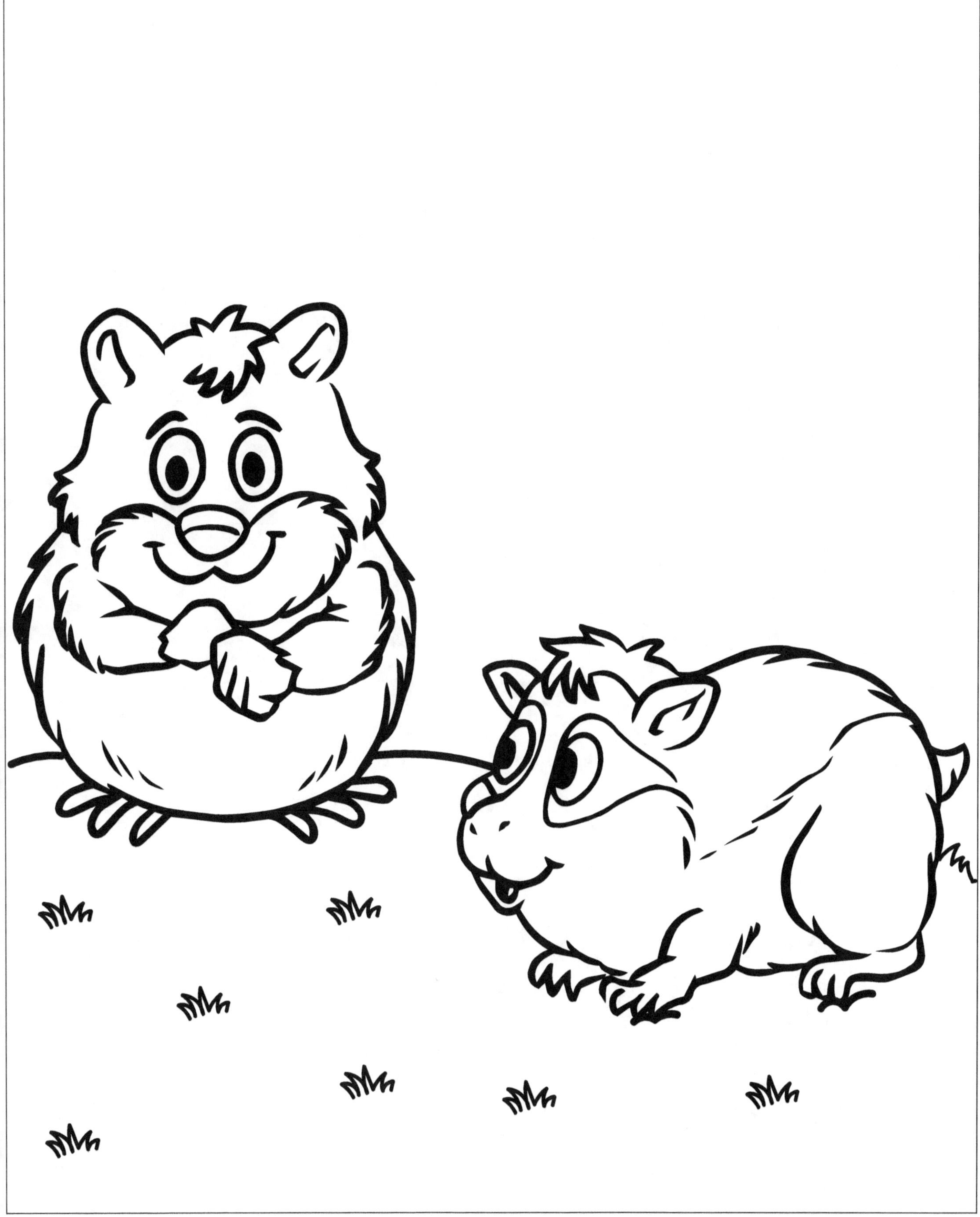

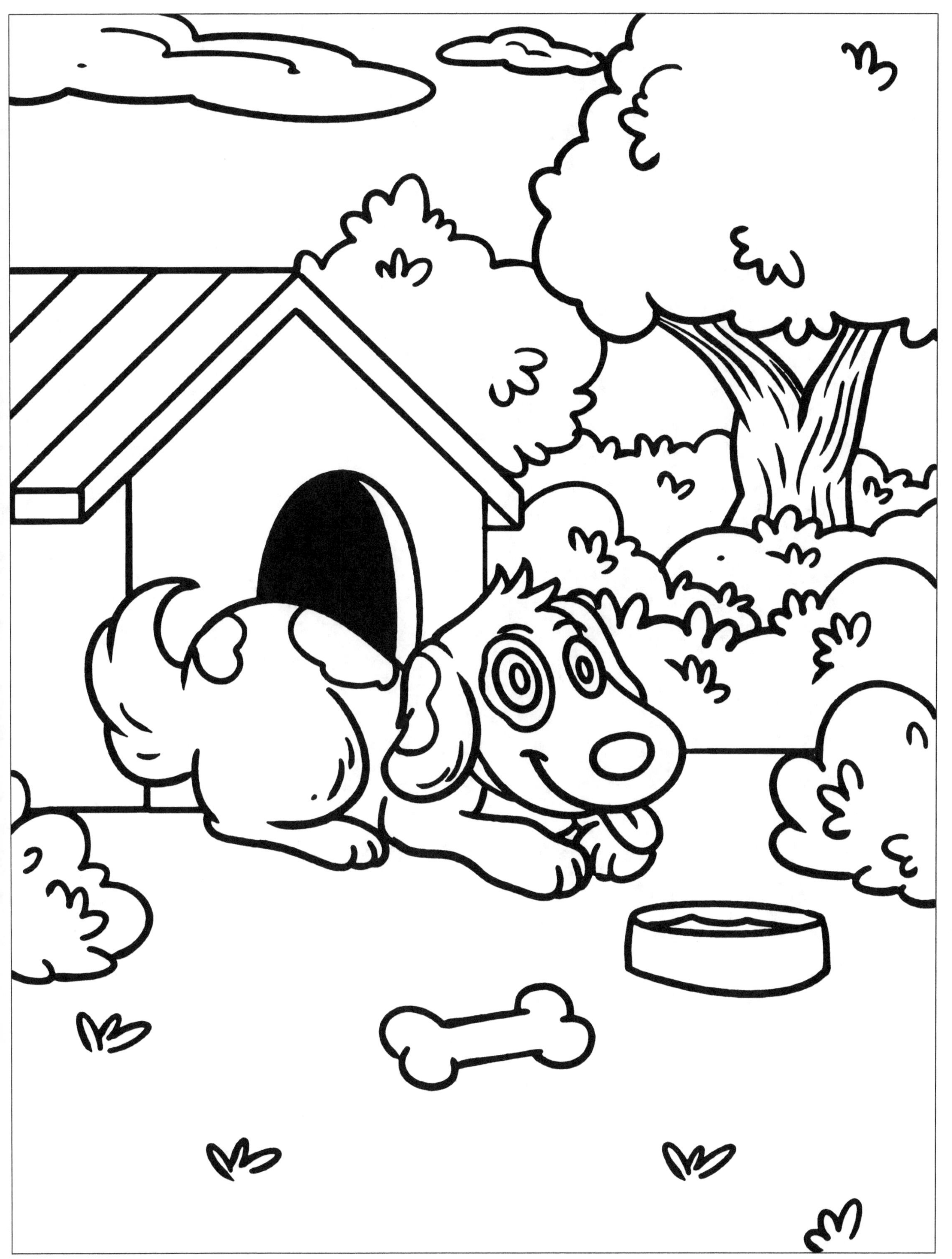

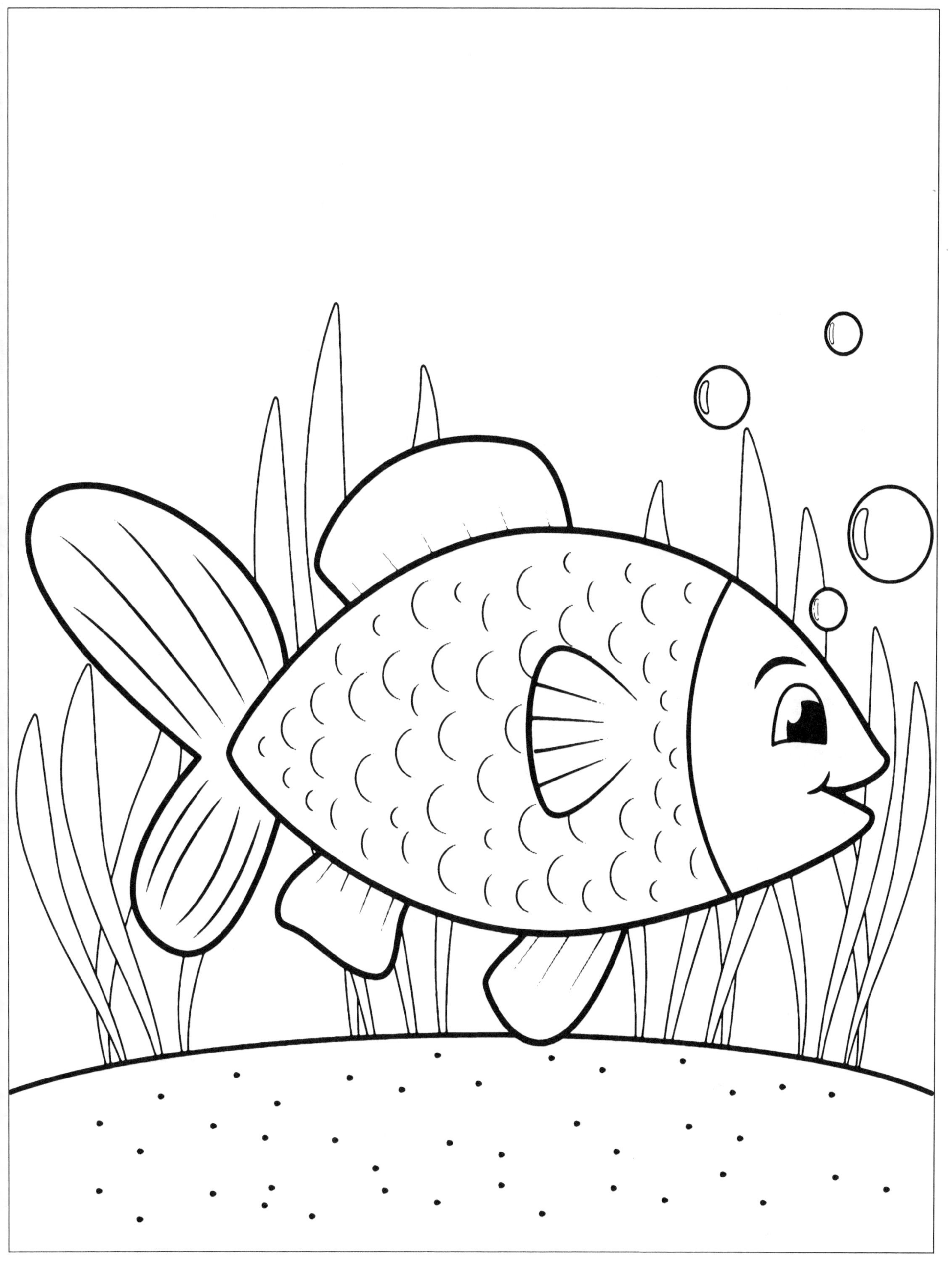

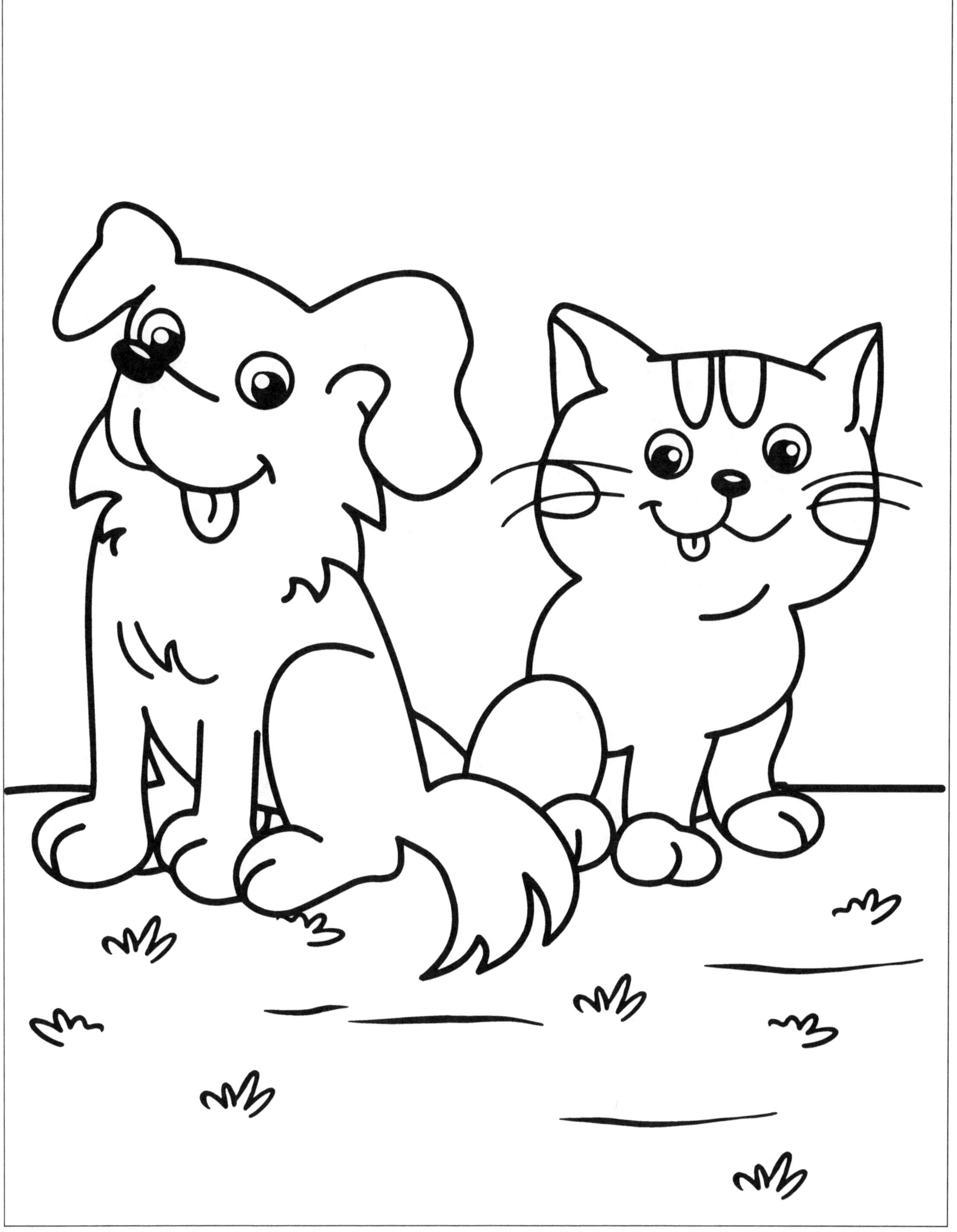

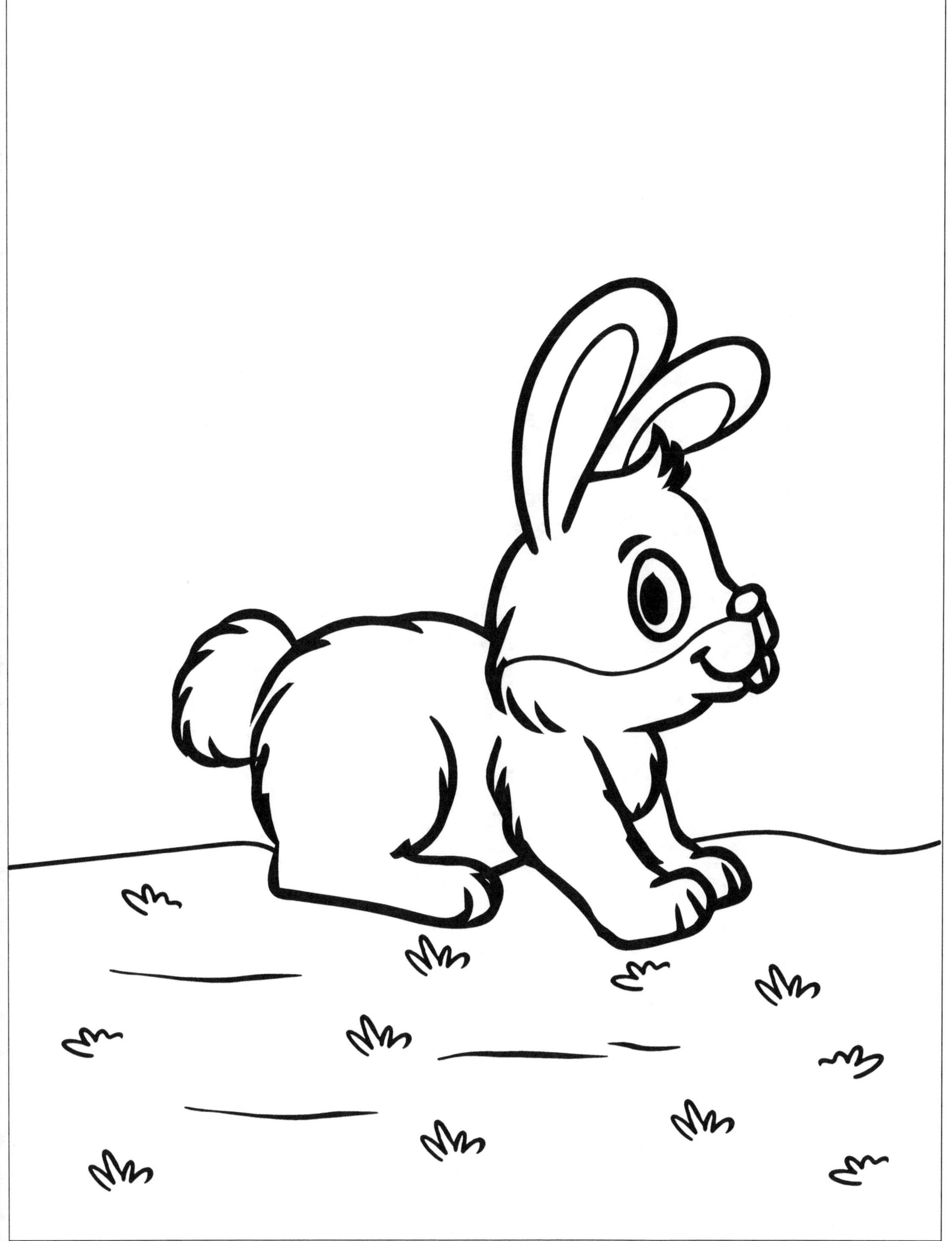

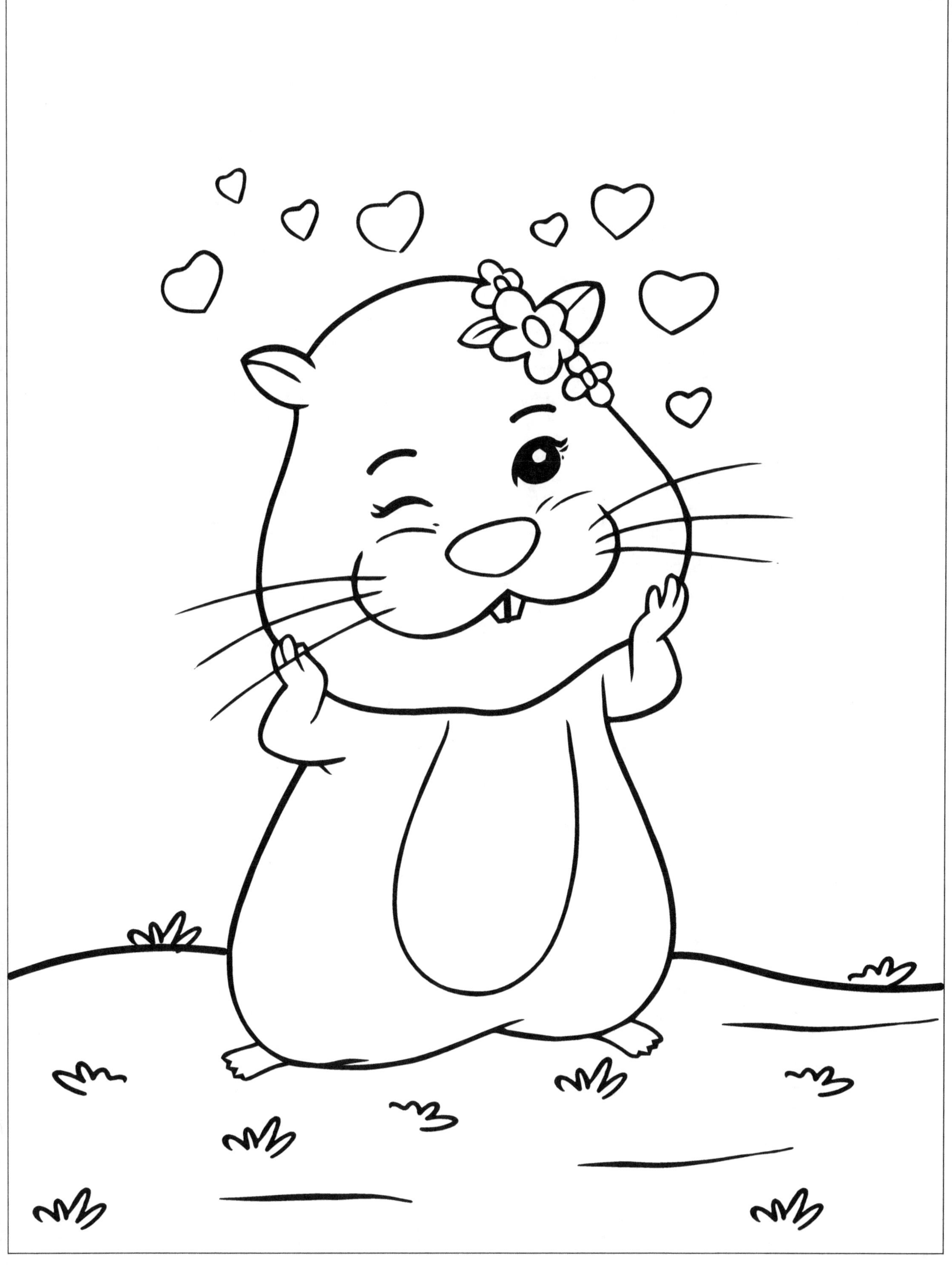

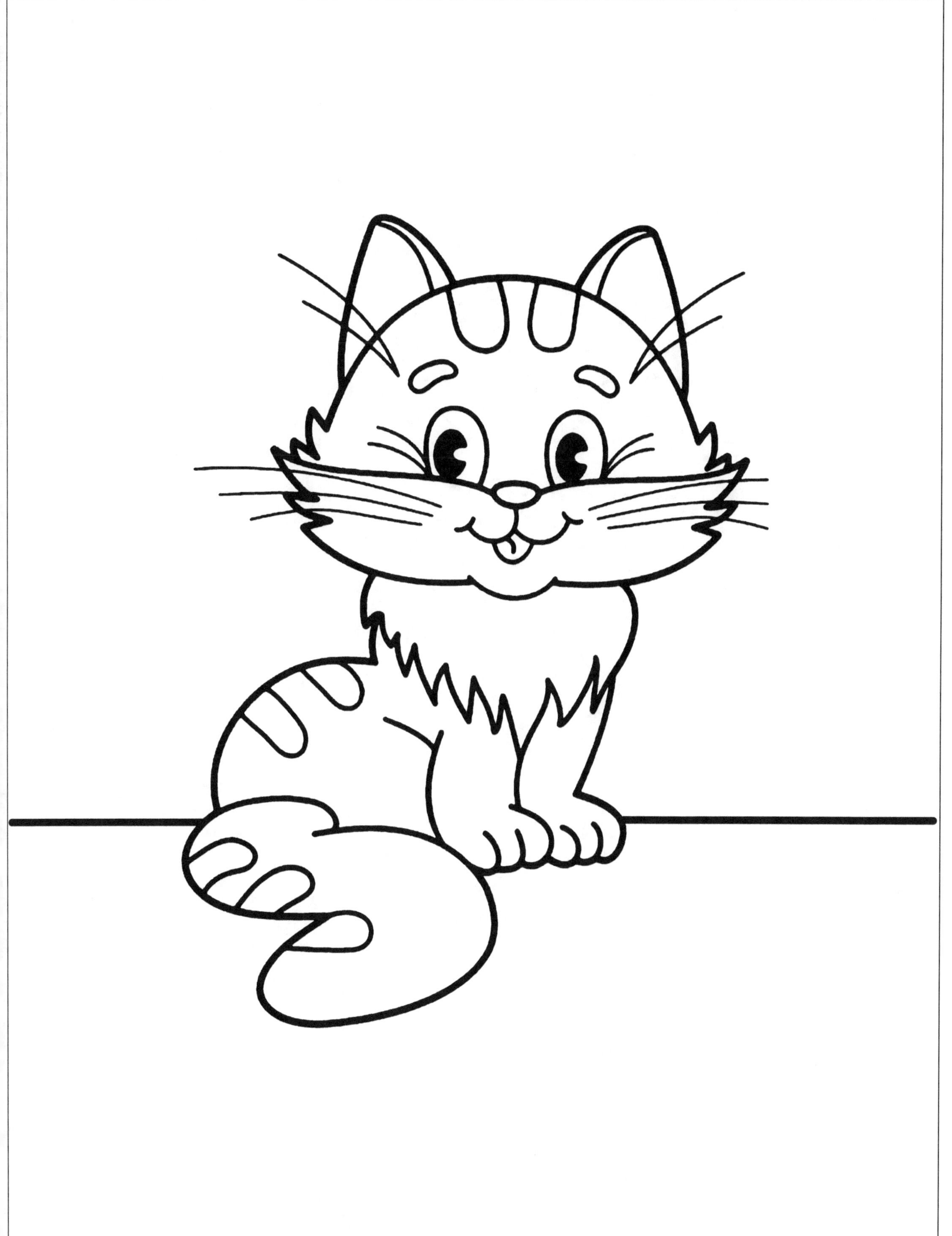

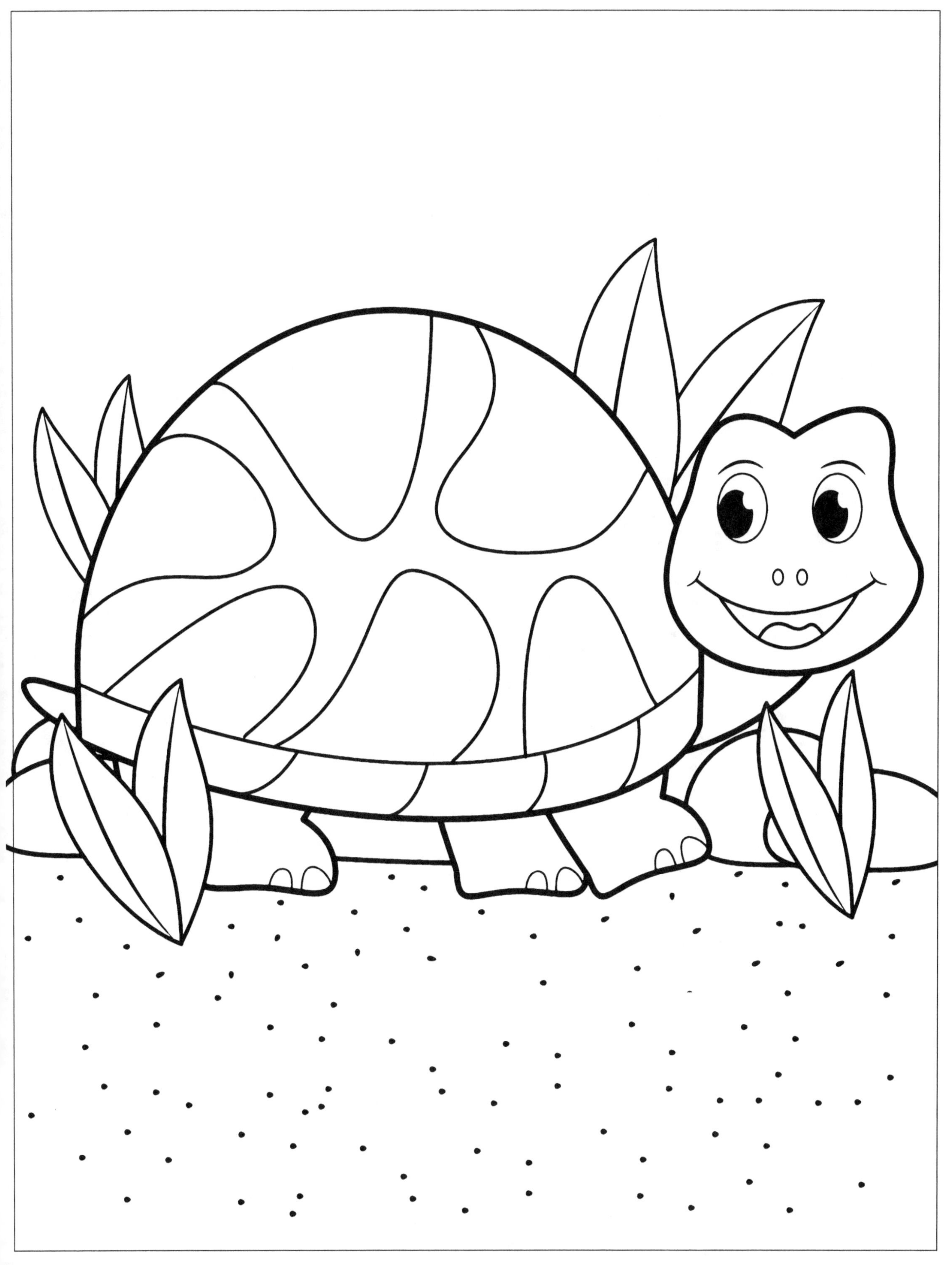

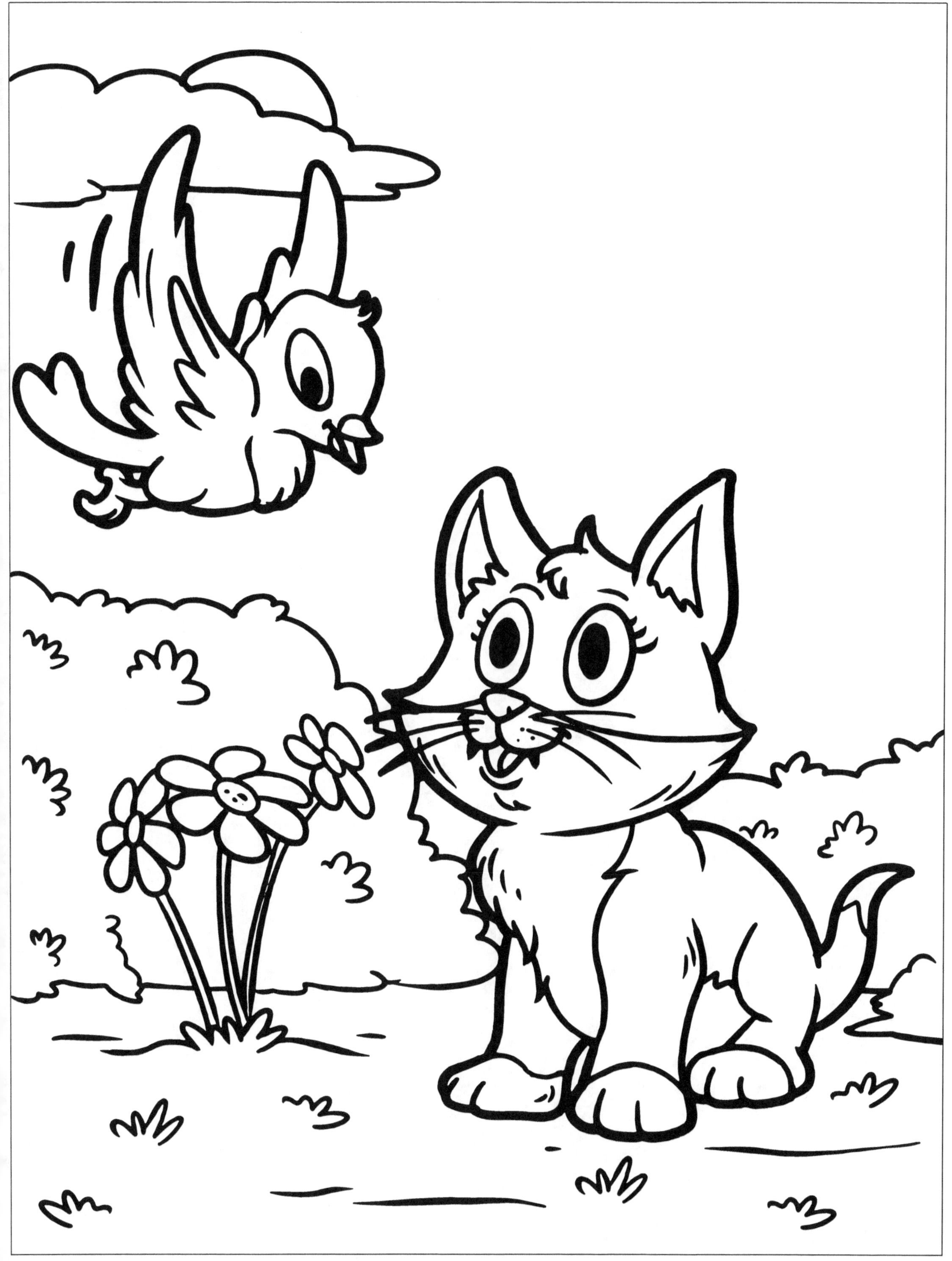

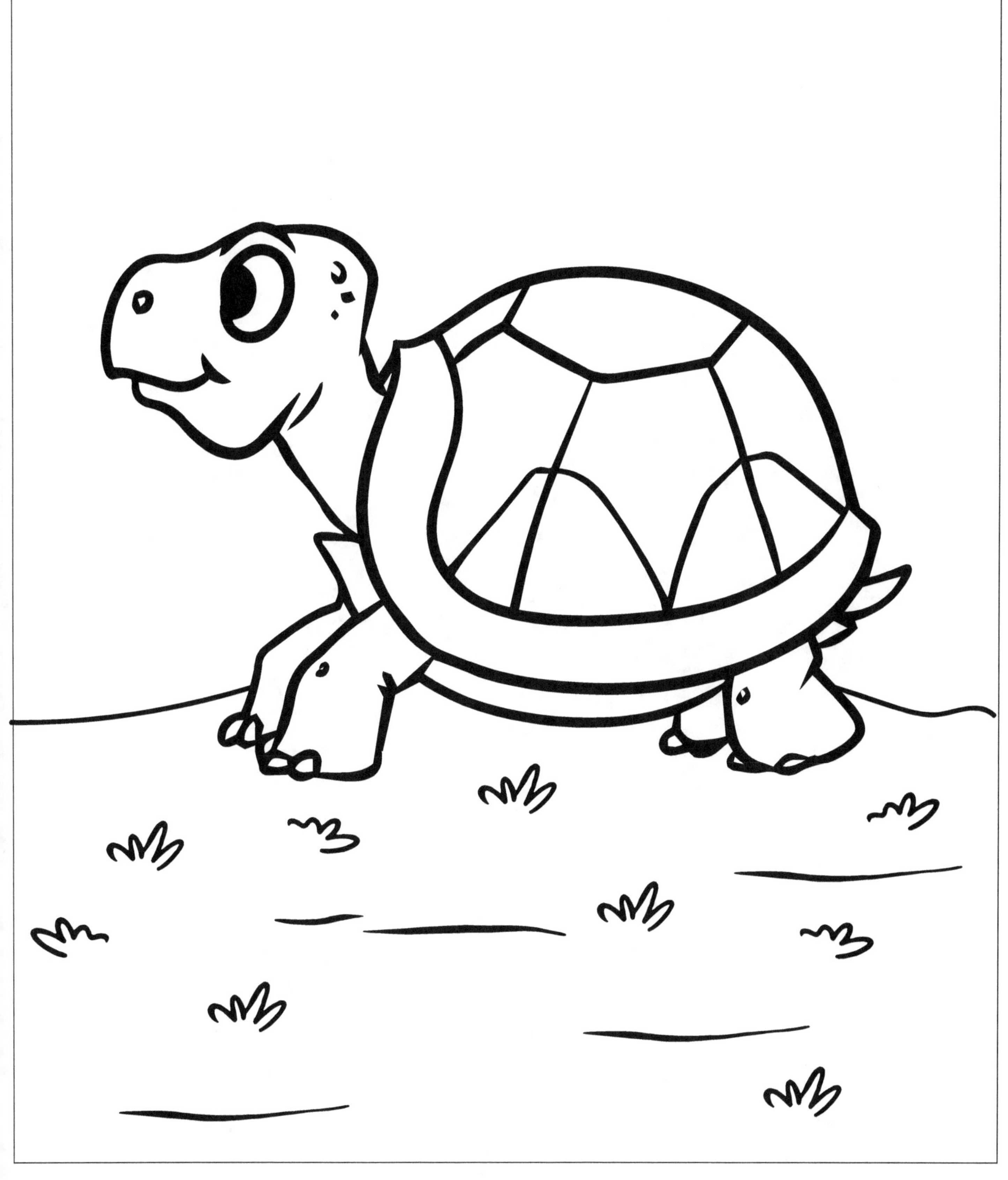

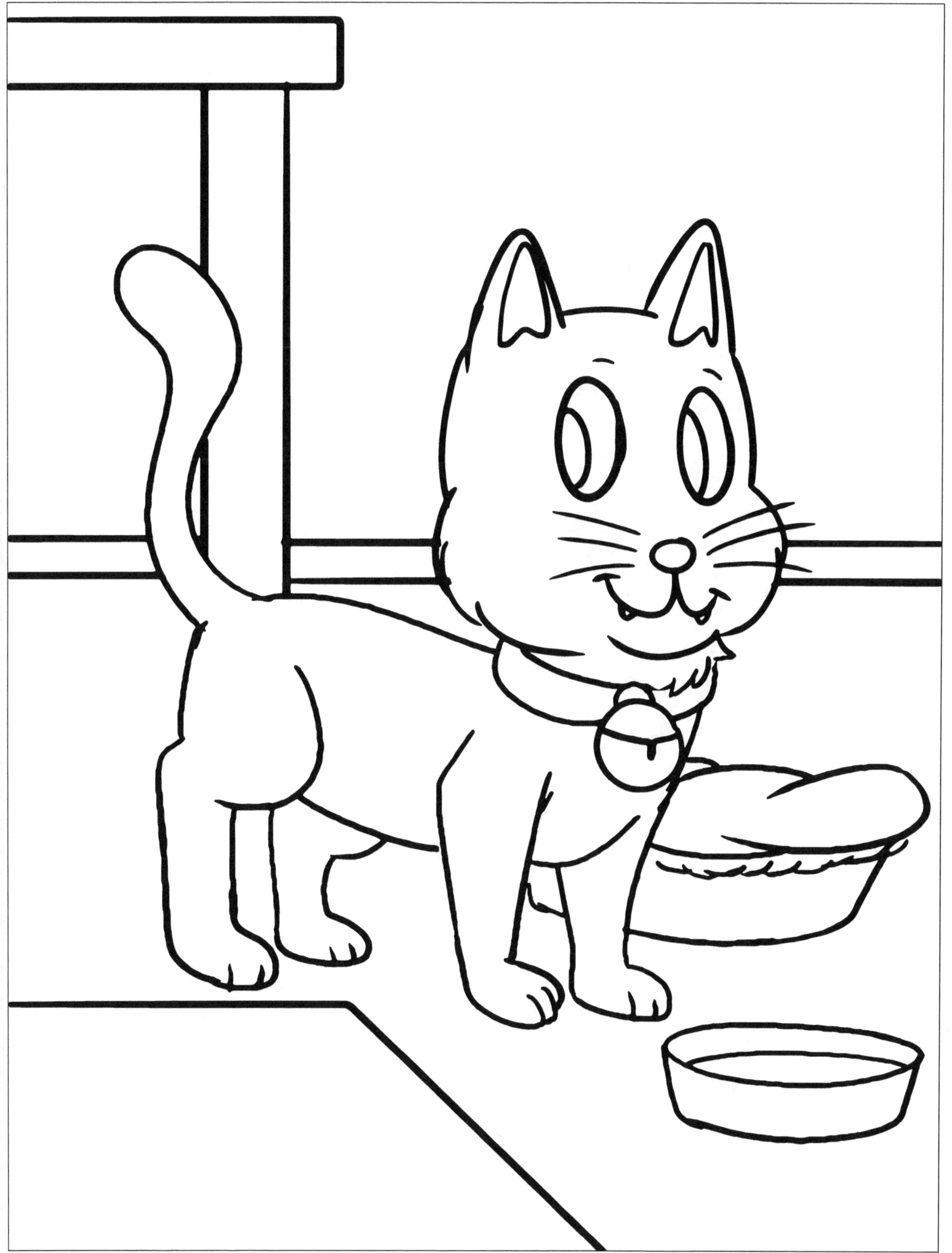

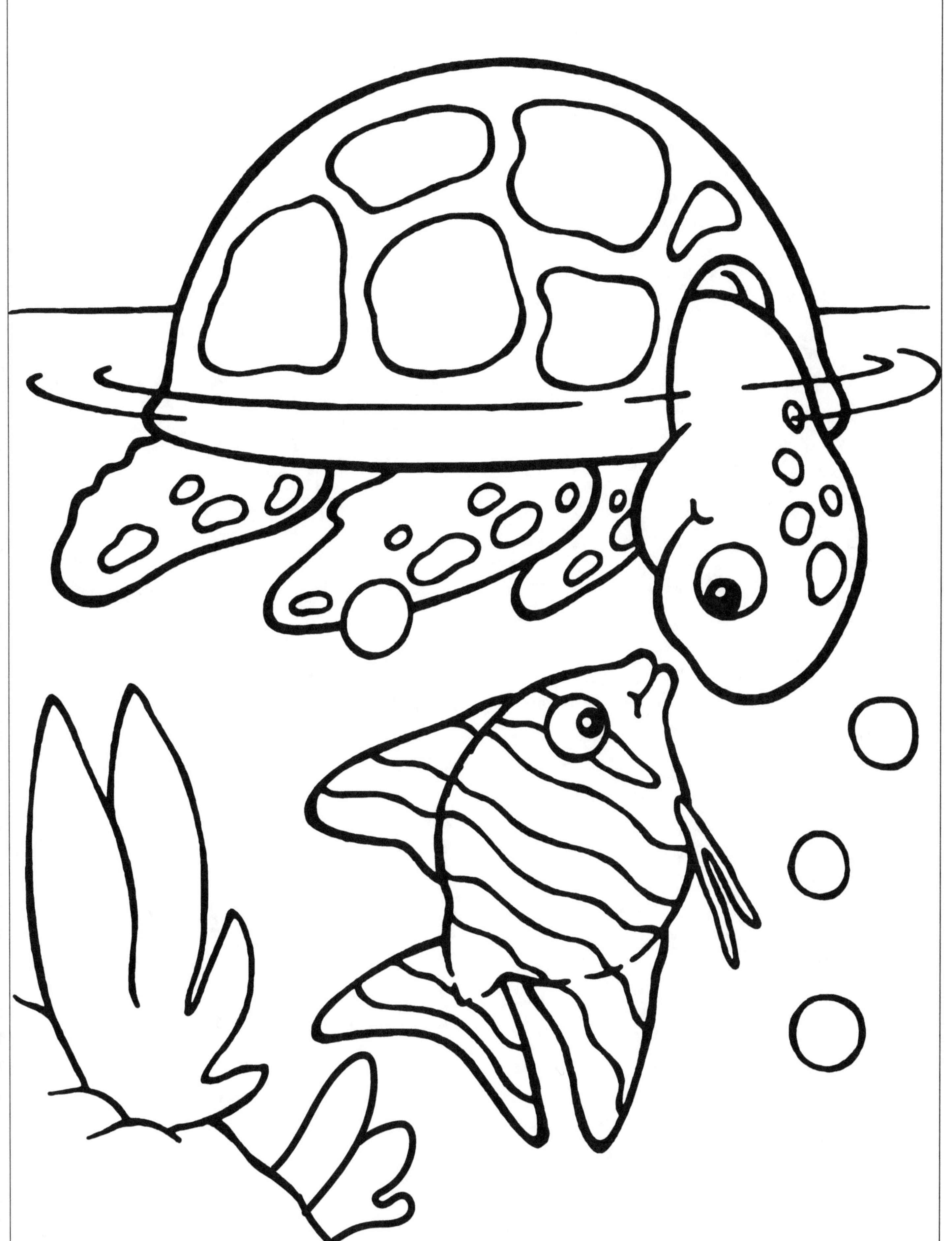

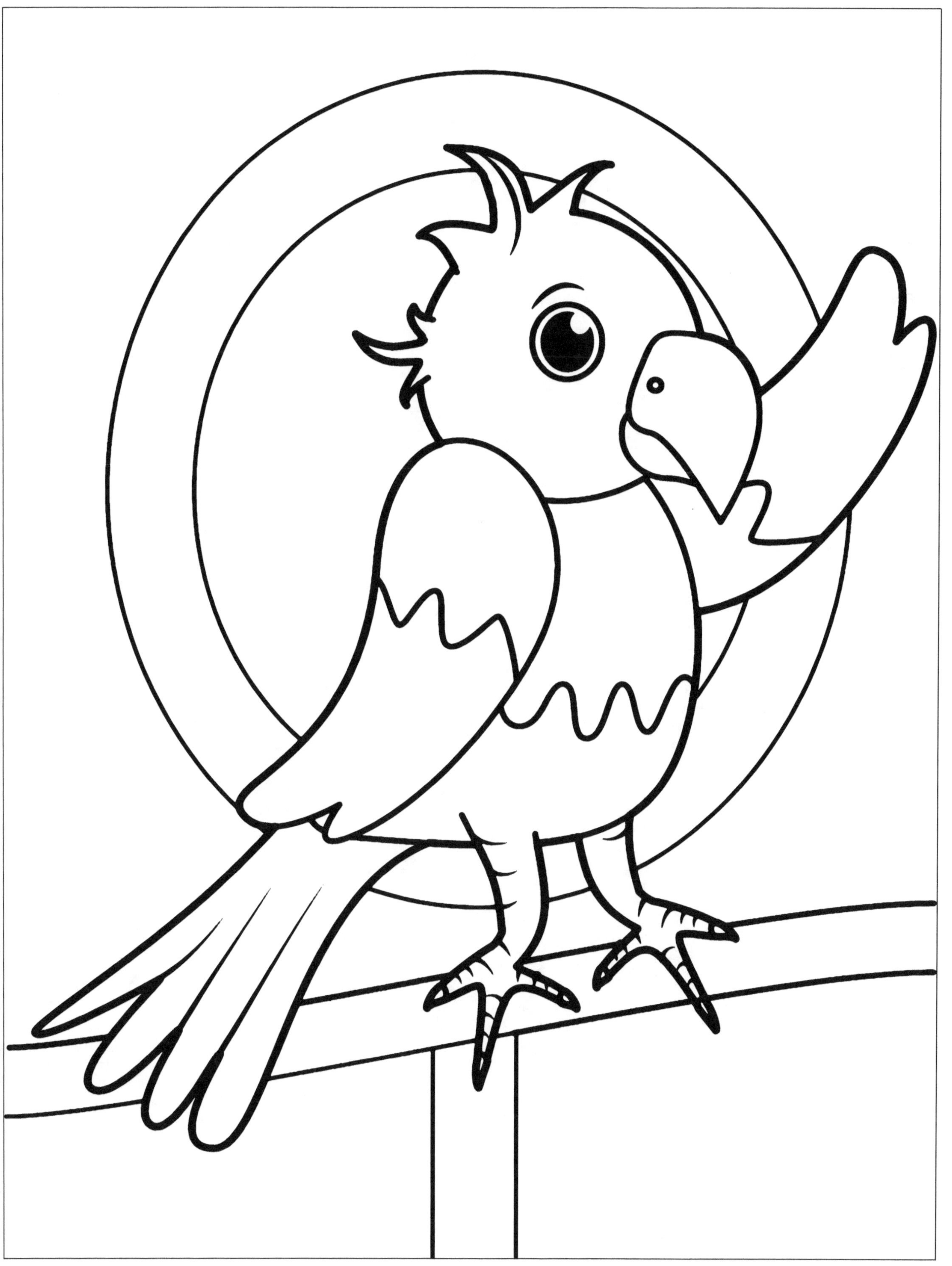

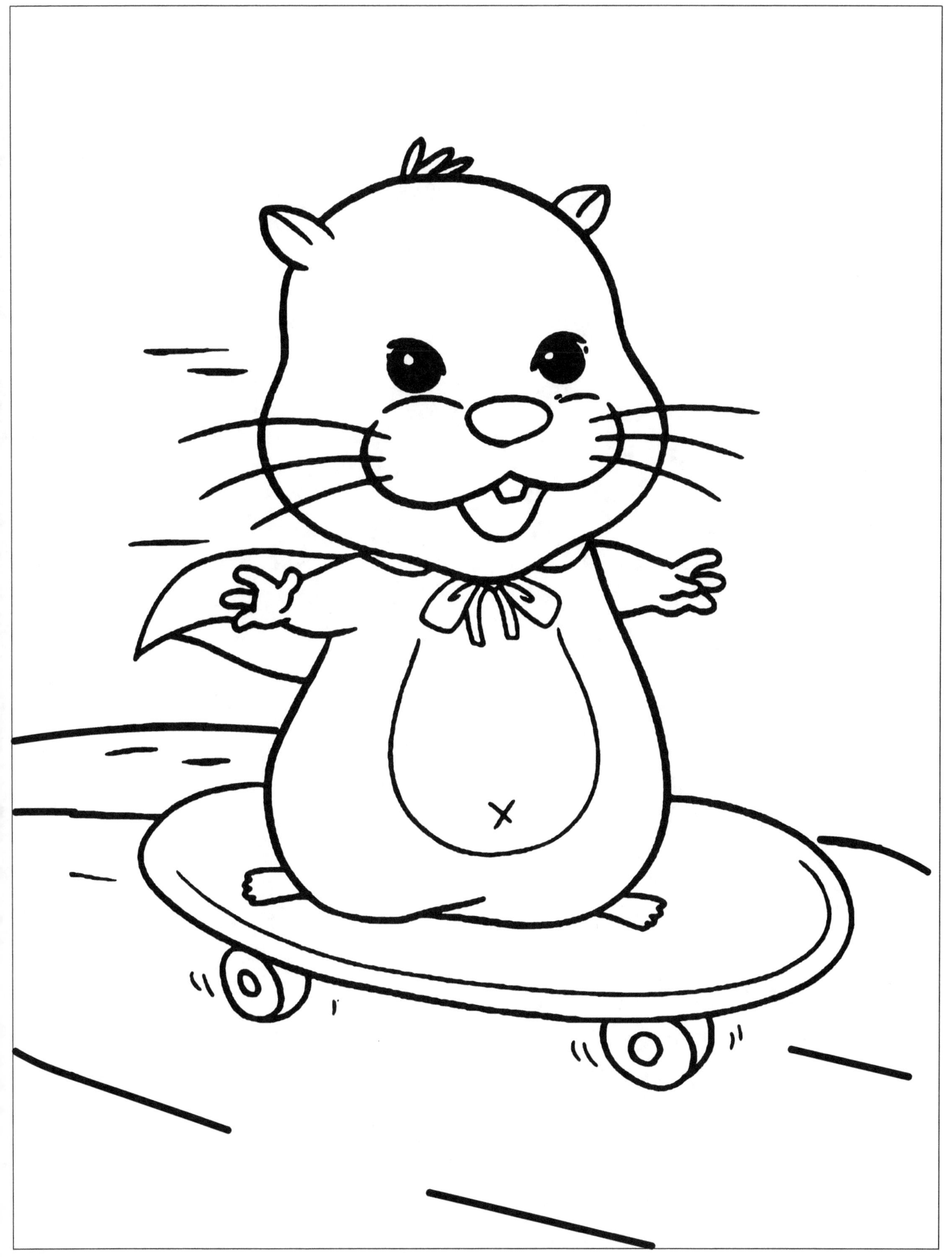

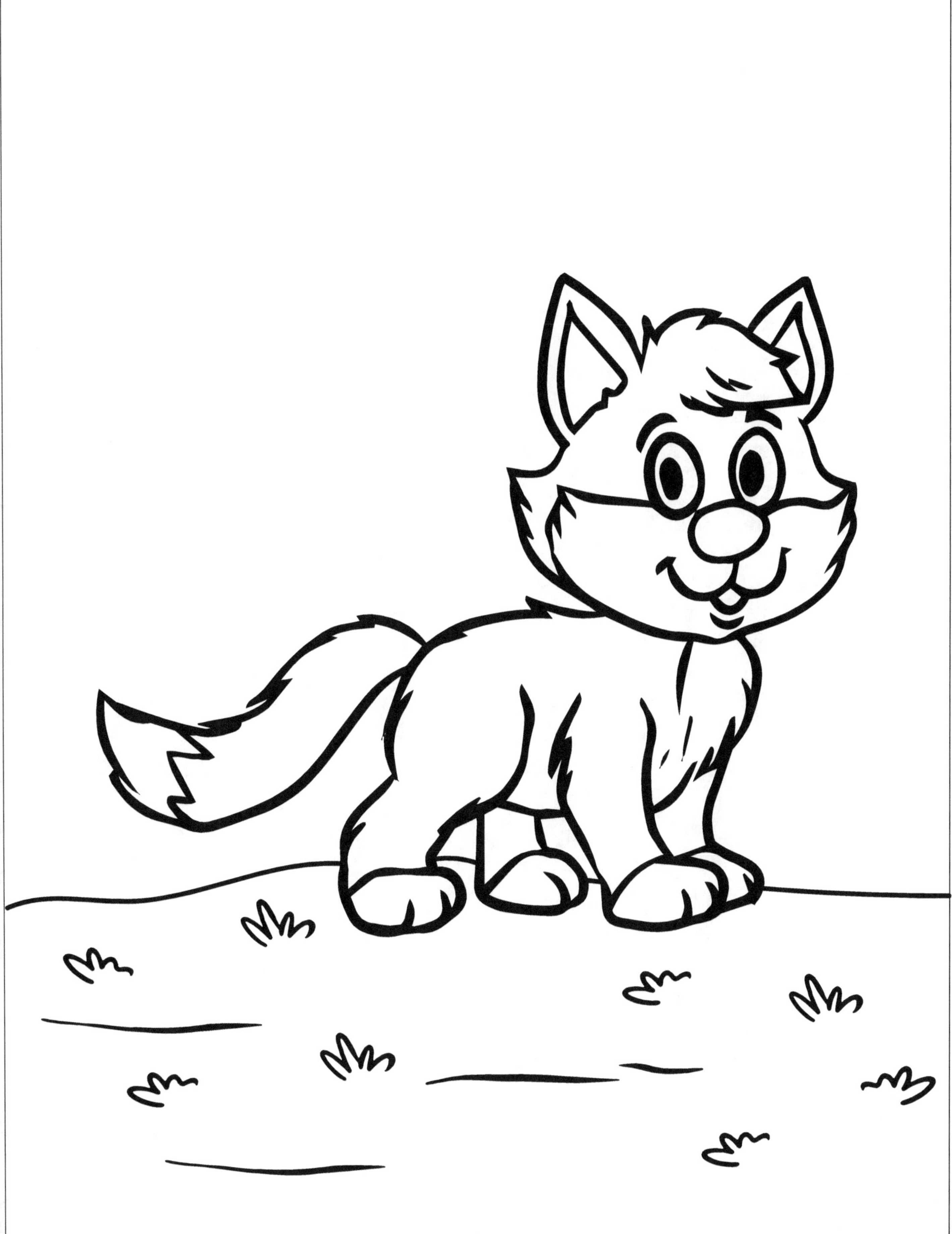

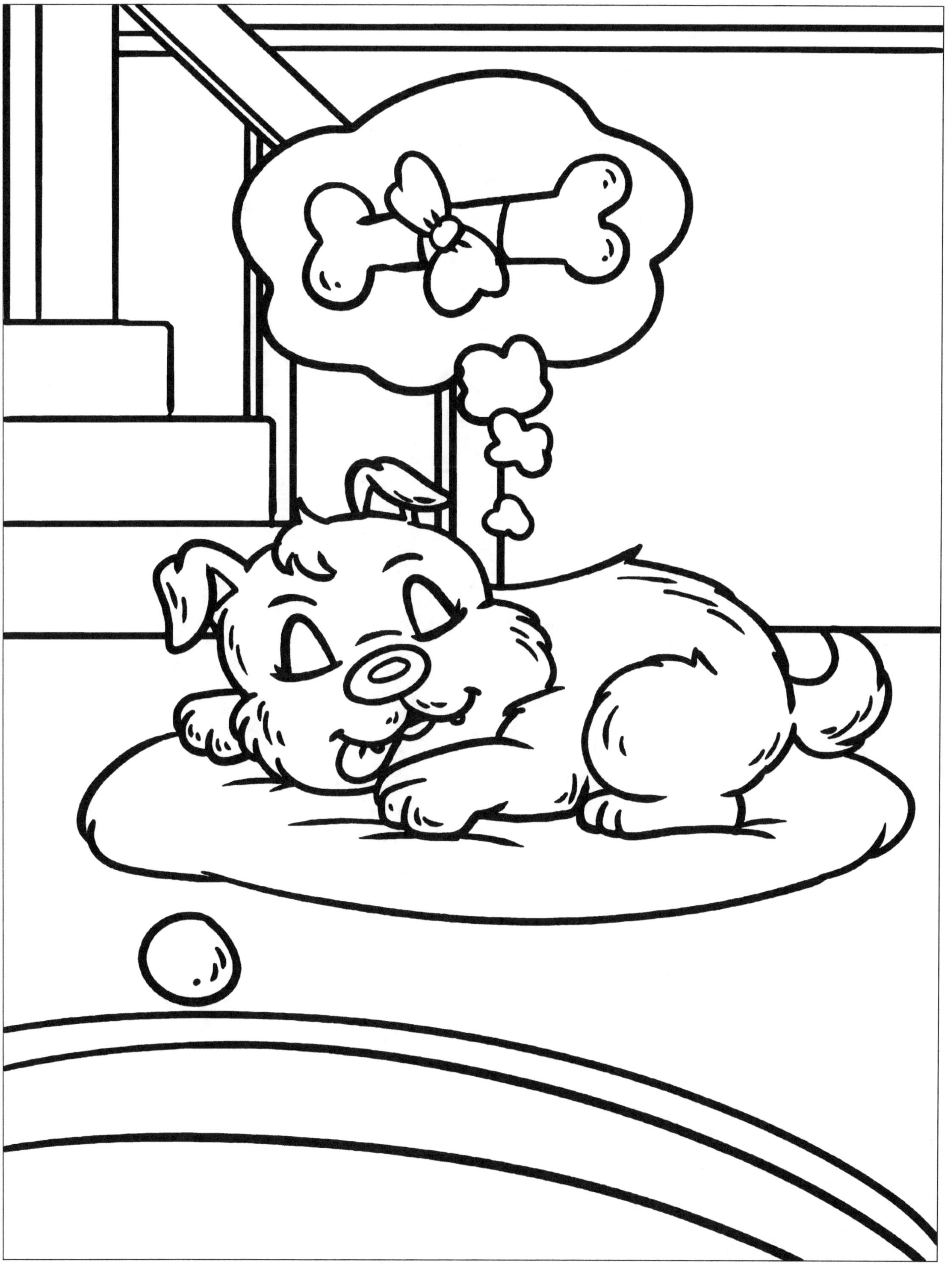

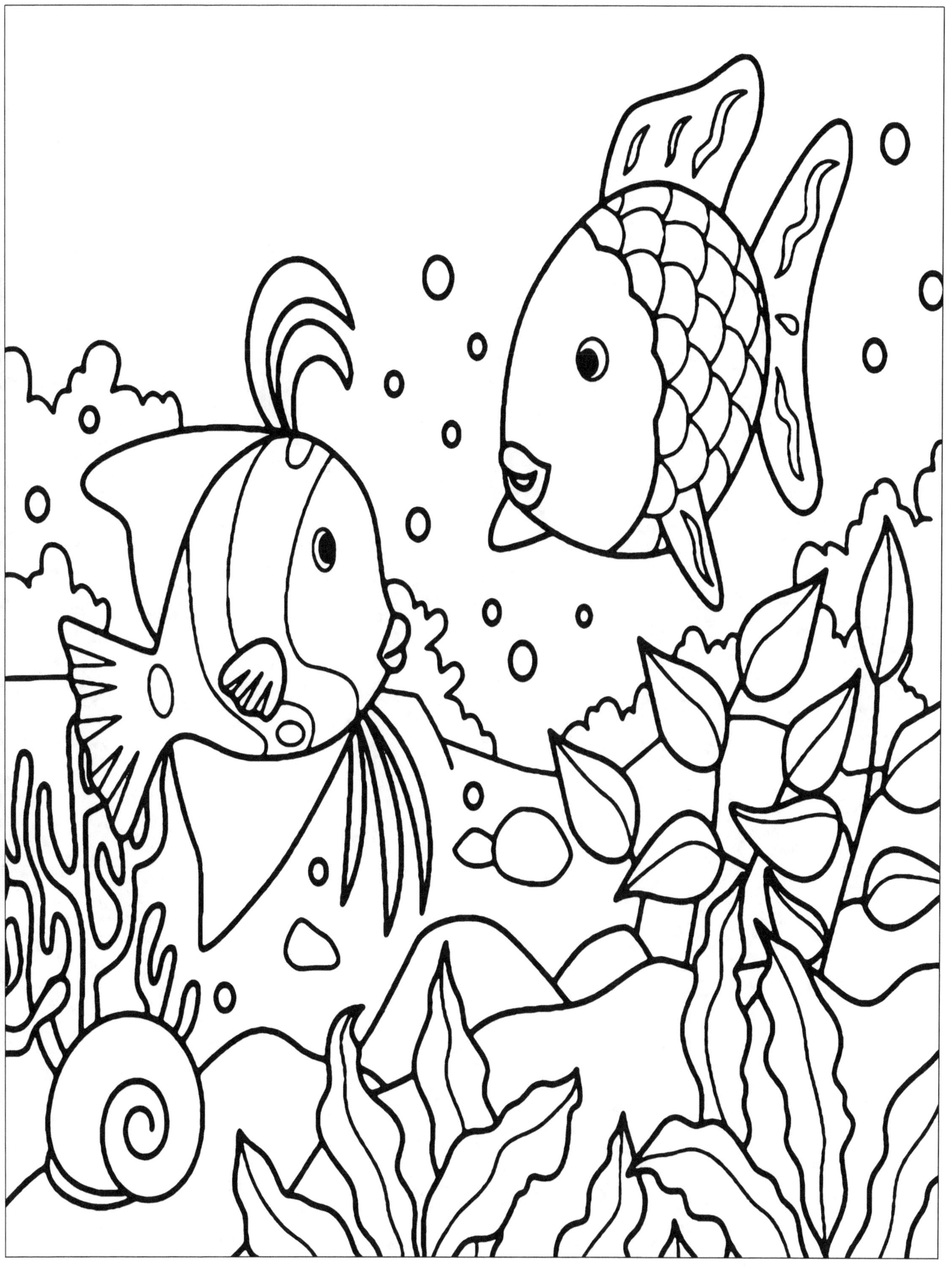

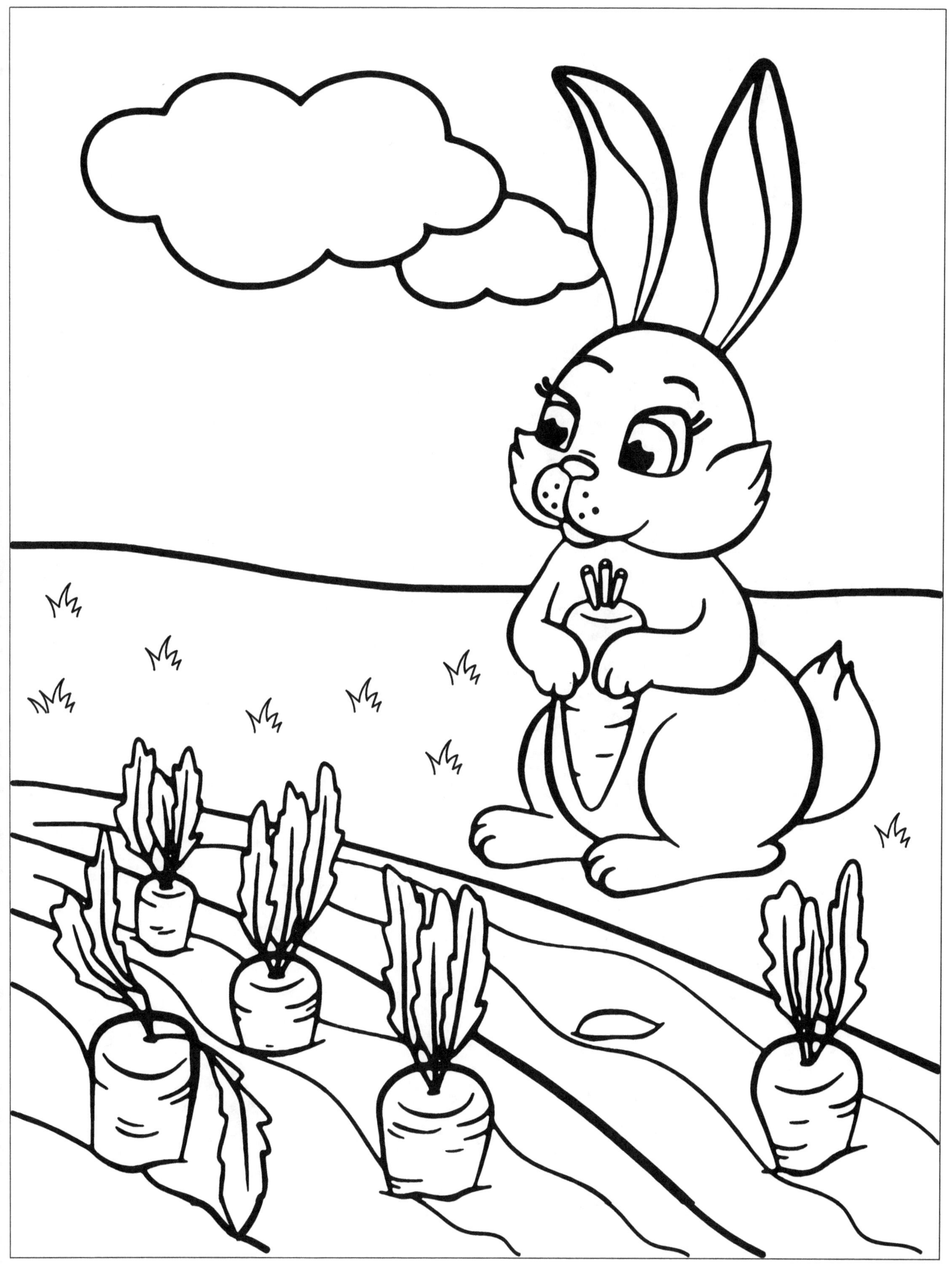

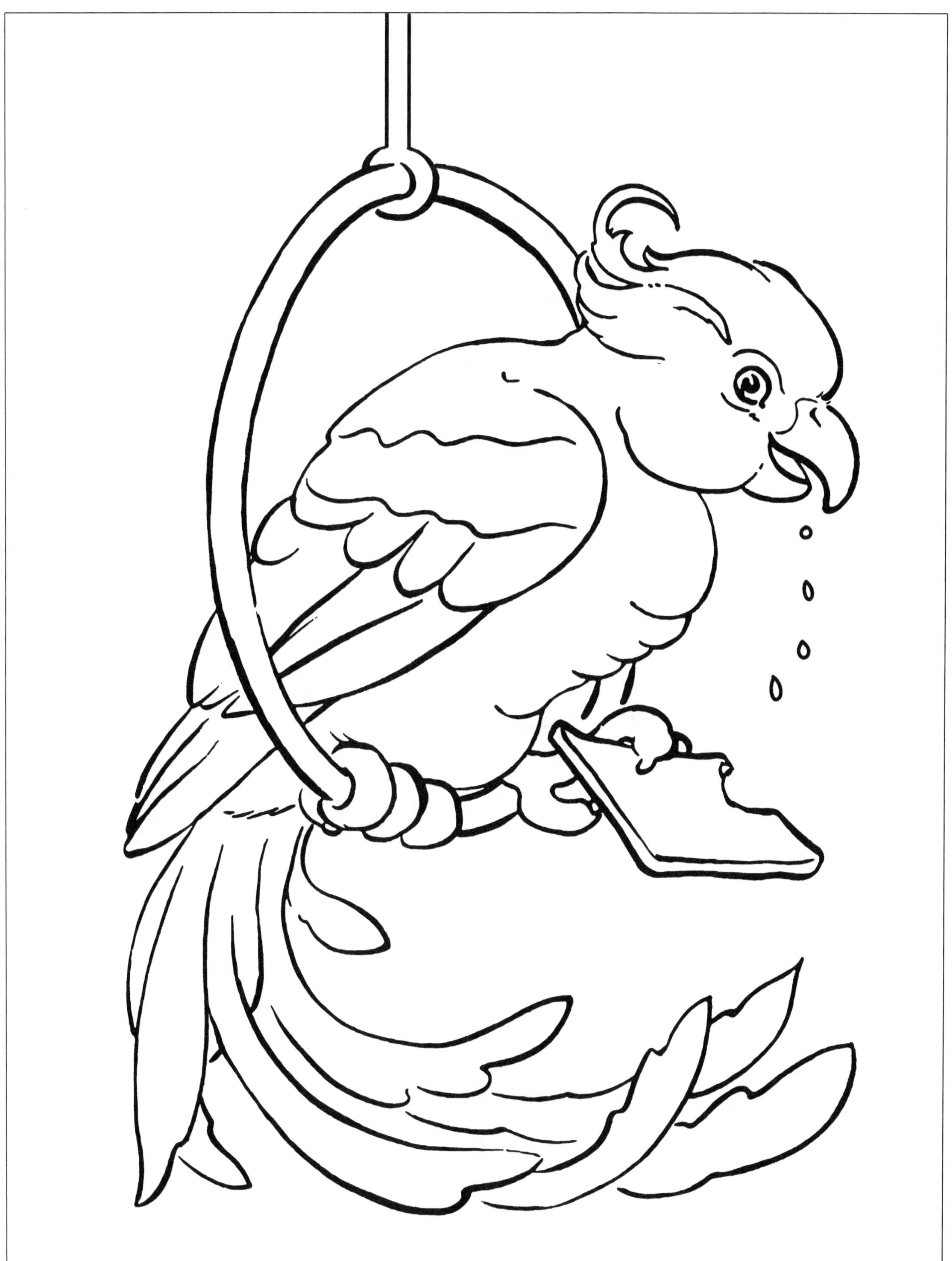

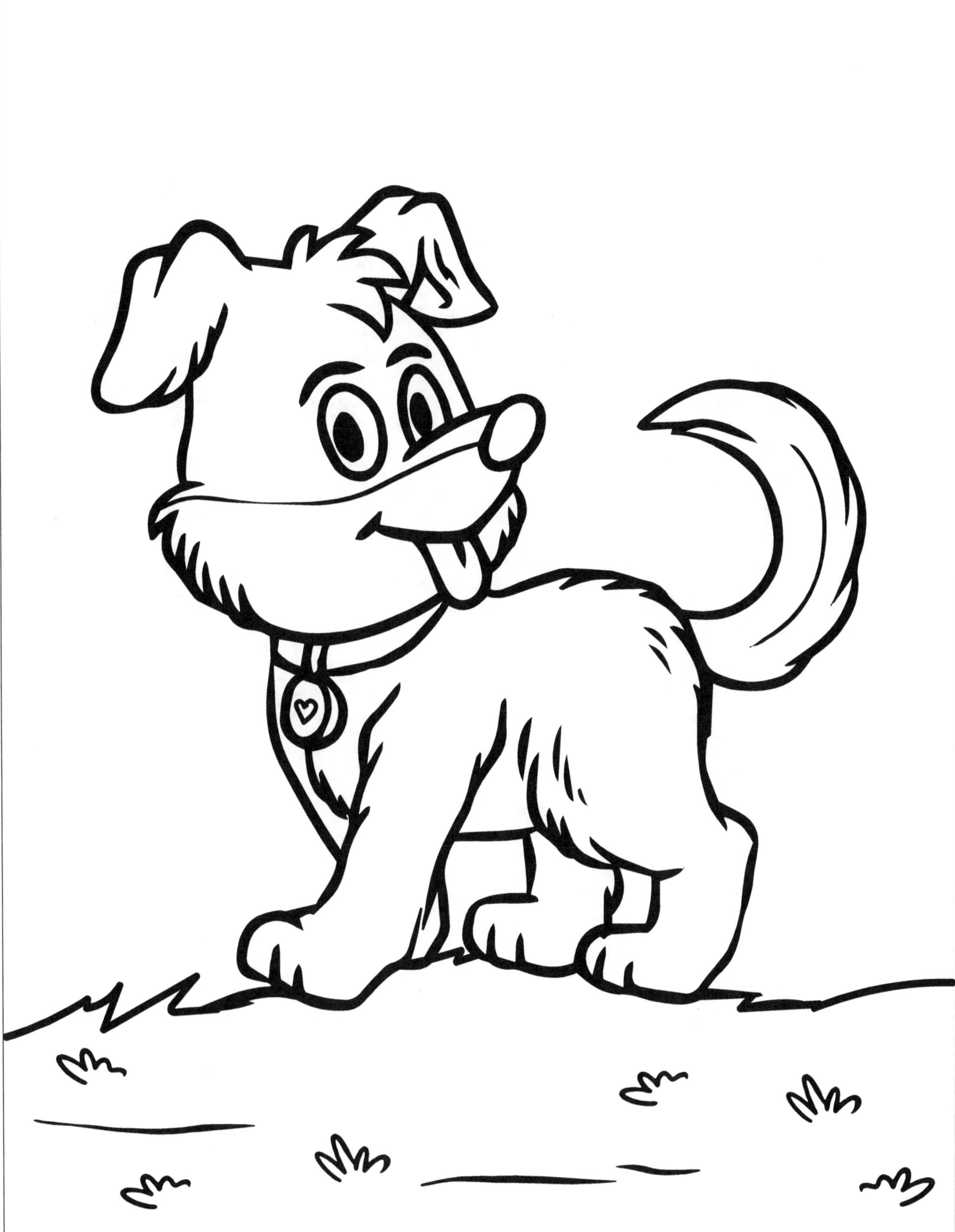

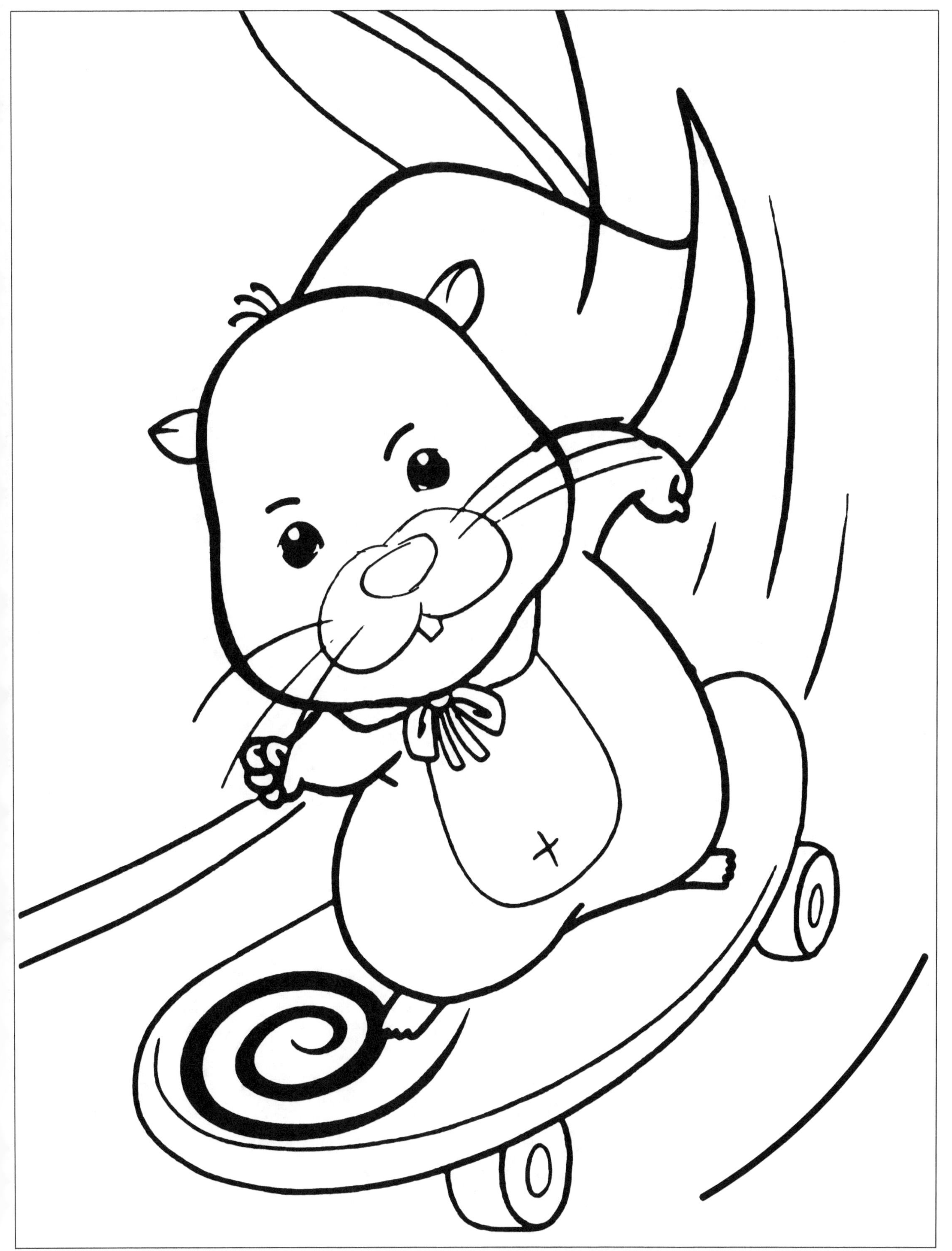

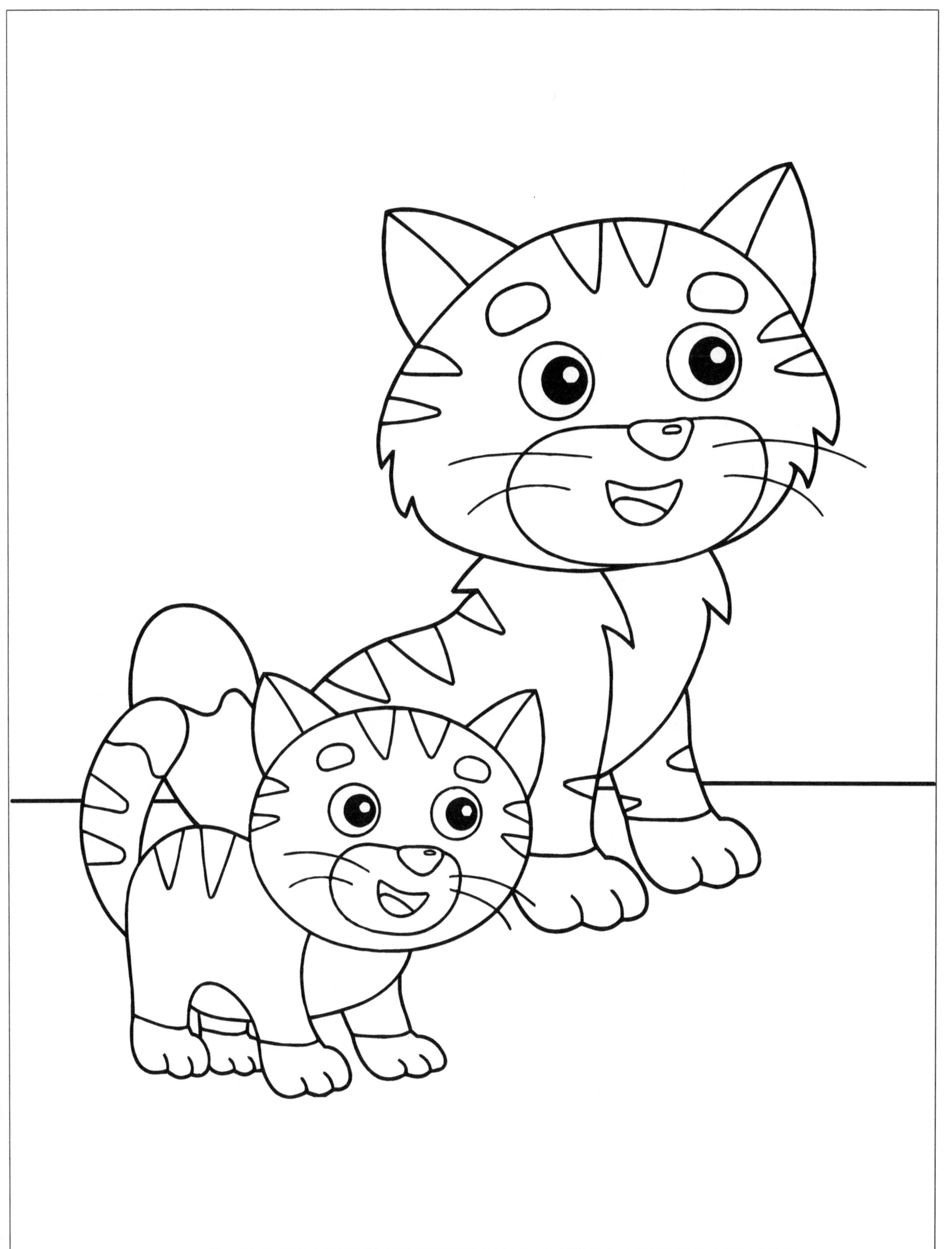

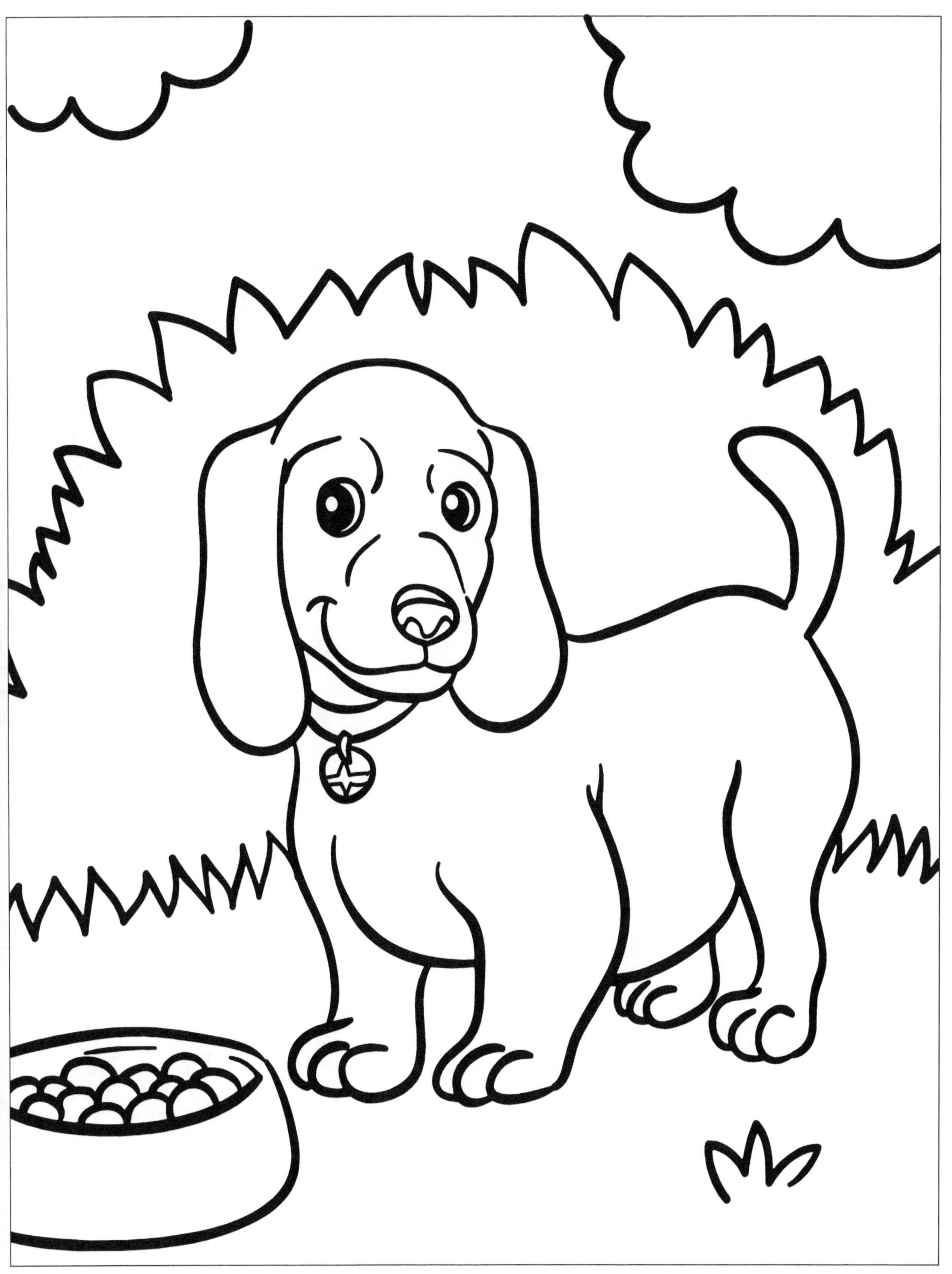

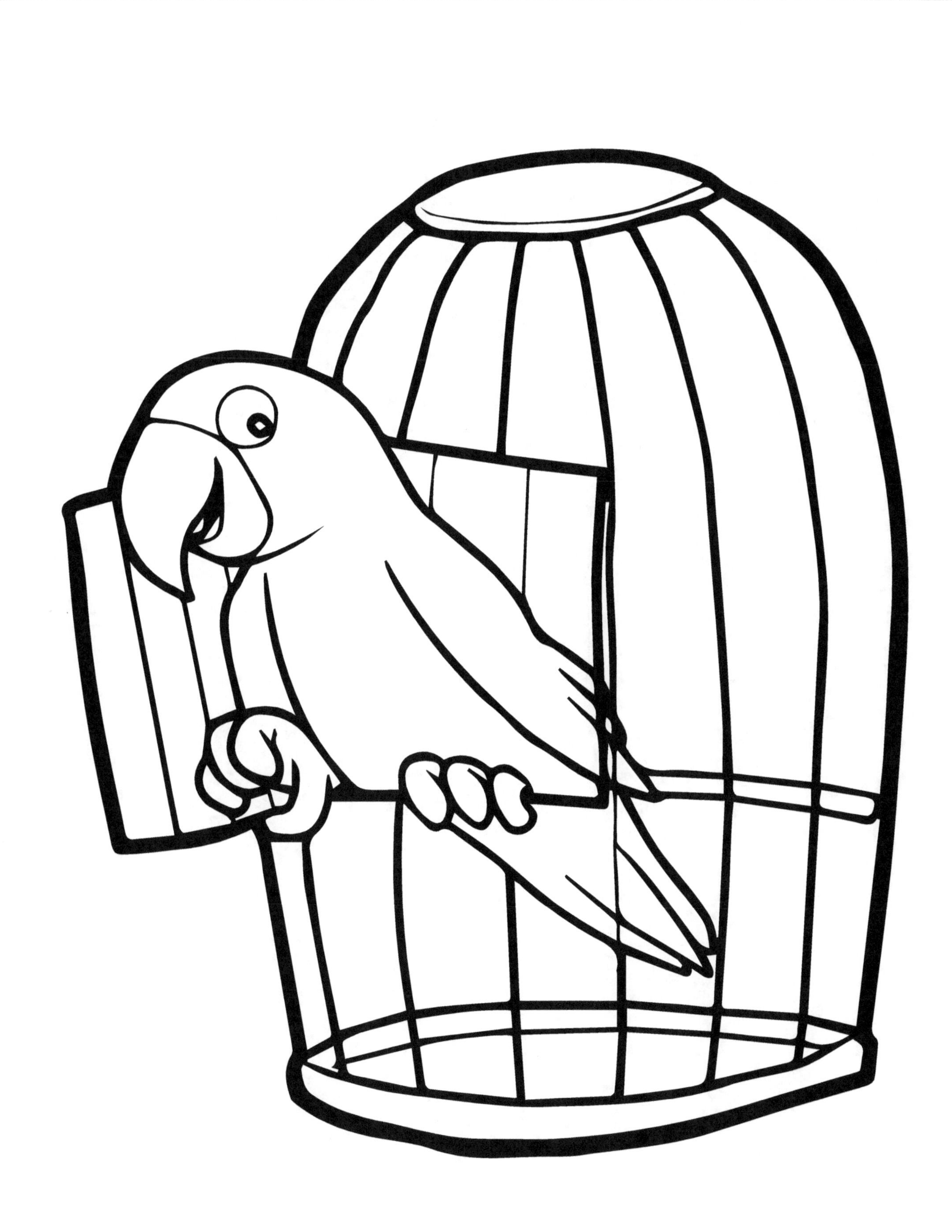

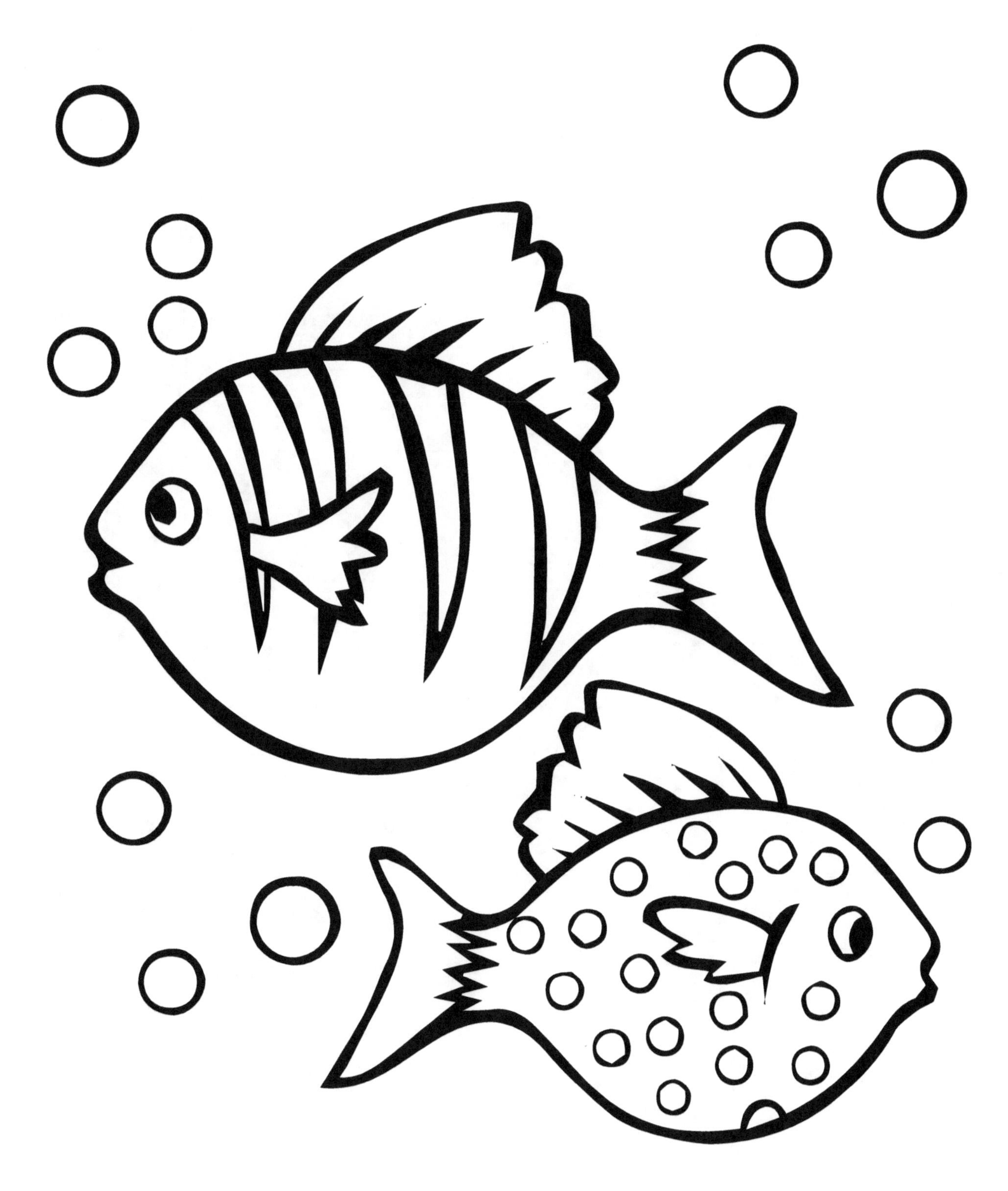

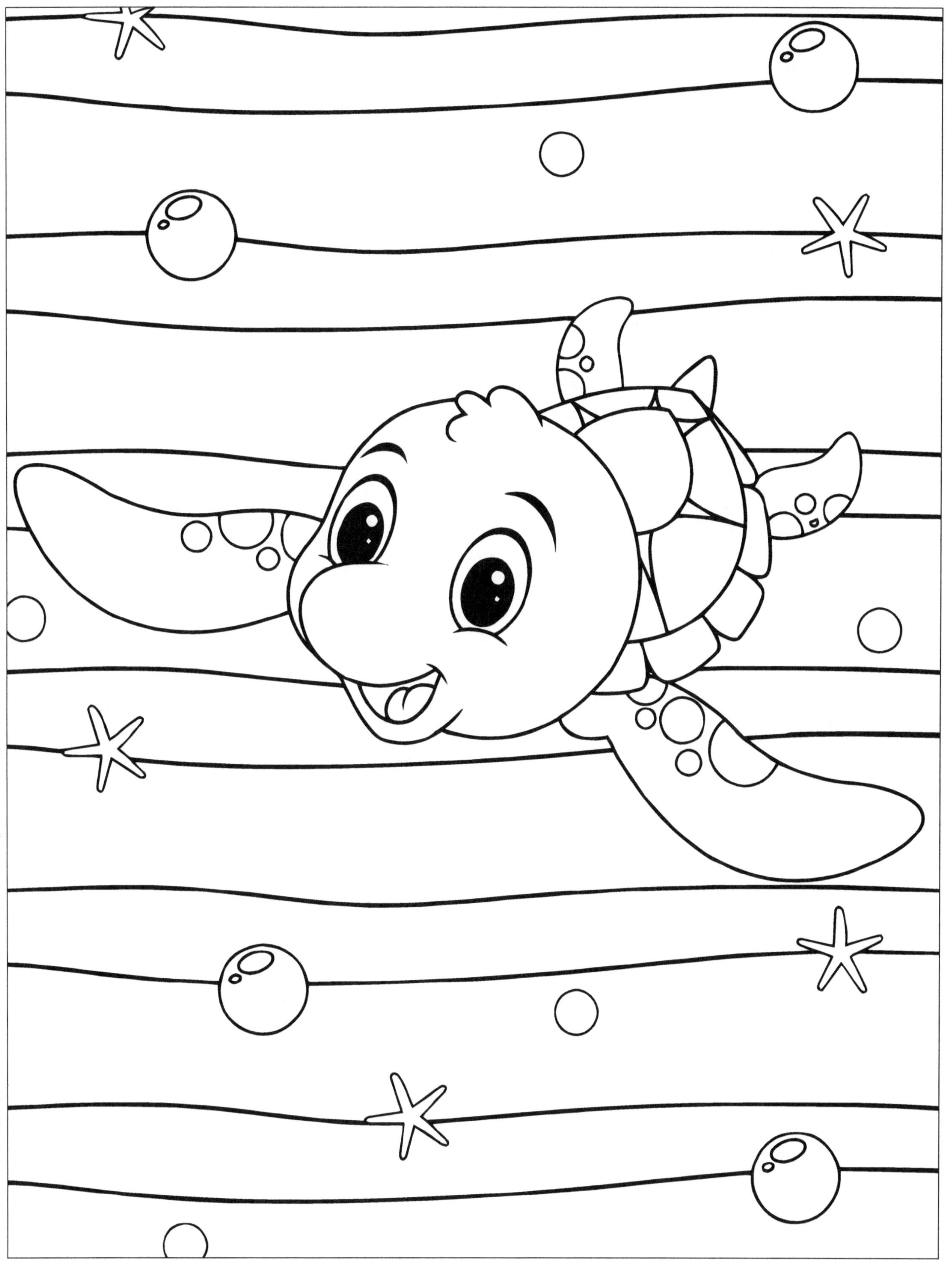

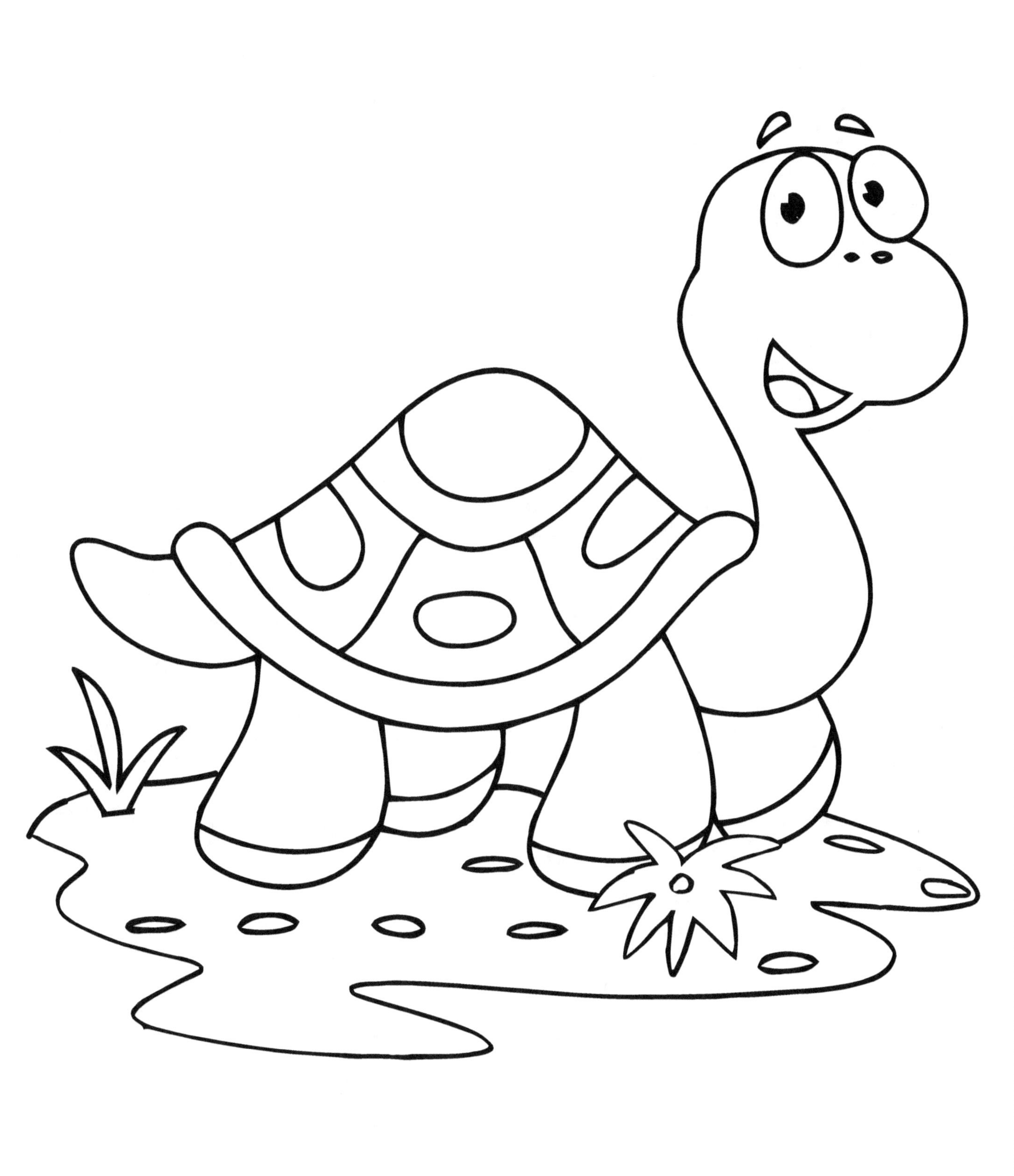

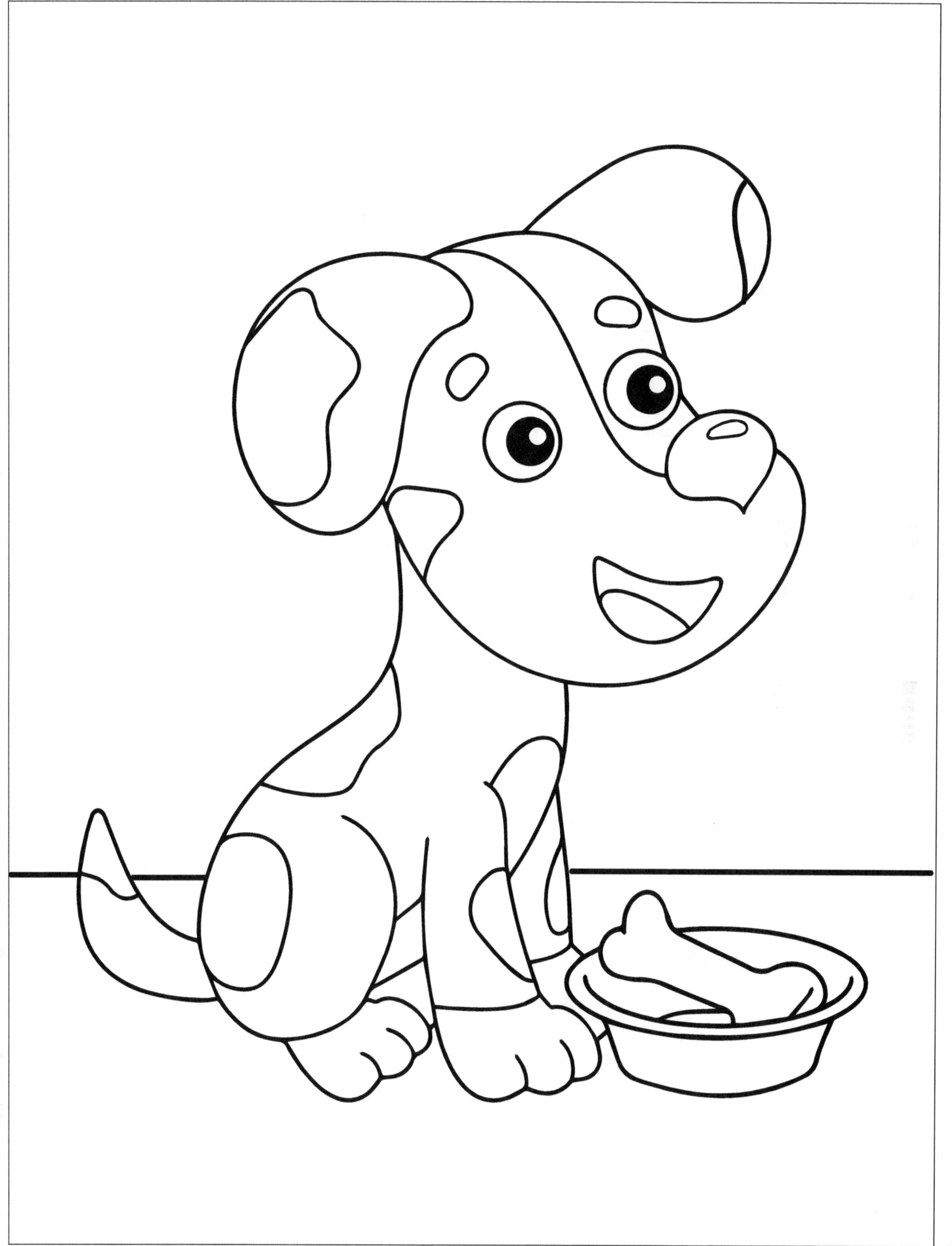

www.ingramcontent.com/pod-product-compliance
Lightning Source LLC
LaVergne TN
LVHW061255100826
845148LV00008B/1138

* 9 7 8 1 7 3 6 5 8 0 8 2 0 *